THE MEANING OF TRAVEL

EMILY THOMAS is Associate Professor in Philosophy at Durham University. She holds a PhD from the University of Cambridge, and worked in the Netherlands before arriving at Durham. Outside the philosophy of travel, she has published extensively on space and time in the history of metaphysics; her scholarly books include *Absolute Time: Rifts in Early Modern Metaphysics*. She has spent several years travelling by herself, getting lost around the world.

Praise for *The Meaning of Travel*

'this profound little book explores why humans choose to wander from their homes with no ostensible purpose other than to make the excursion in question. [Thomas] takes on the task of explaining it with a verve and lilt that are rare in modern professors.'

The Wall Street Journal

'Thomas has used her command of the philosophical canon to extend our understanding of an impulse that many of us share but few examine in such depth. *The Meaning of Travel* is a manifesto for the virtues that travel can bestow on the traveller — not just an increase in knowledge, but a deep humility at the scale and diversity of the world, and an enduring wonder that we live on such a planet.'

The Spectator

'The byways and highways of Thomas's subject are well-illuminated. Delineating, direct and droll by turns...Novelty, knowledge and insight can be found in travel. It can make us wiser as well as better-informed...having read this book, I am now both.'

Standpoint Magazine

'No one could ask for a more congenial companion than Emily Thomas on her 2,000-plus year journey through *The Meaning of Travel* for major Western philosophers from Plato to Simone de Beauvoir...*The Meaning of Travel* succeeds in offering an engaging primer on how travel has transformed both what we know and how we think.'

Times Higher Education "Book of the Week"

'This is the finest kind of travel: not just across continents, but through time, space and our infinite minds. The journey is the joy, and Emily Thomas a terrific guide.'

Mike Parker, author of *Map Addict*

'At last – a book not about where we travel, but why. *The Meaning of Travel* illuminates the reasons we've been tempted to set out on untrodden paths for centuries.'

Dea Birkett, author of *Serpent in Paradise*

'Brilliantly researched and detailed, while staying humorous throughout, "*The Meaning of Travel*" is a fantastic exploration of how travel can broaden the mind.'

Much Better Adventures

philosophers abroad

THE MEANING OF TRAVEL

EMILY **THOMAS**

OXFORD
UNIVERSITY PRESS

OXFORD

UNIVERSITY PRESS

Great Clarendon Street, Oxford, OX2 6DP,
United Kingdom

Oxford University Press is a department of the University of Oxford.
It furthers the University's objective of excellence in research, scholarship,
and education by publishing worldwide. Oxford is a registered trade mark of
Oxford University Press in the UK and in certain other countries

First published 2020
First published in paperback 2022

Impression: 1

Published in the United States of America by Oxford University Press
198 Madison Avenue, New York, NY 10016, United States of America

British Library Cataloguing in Publication Data
Data available

Library of Congress Cataloging in Publication Data
Data available

ISBN 978–0–19–883540–0 (Hbk.)
ISBN 978–0–19–883541–7 (Pbk.)

Printed and bound in the UK by
Clays Ltd, Elcograf S.p.A.

For Erin, Eva, and Mar

CONTENTS

Contents

LIST OF ILLUSTRATIONS

TRAVELLING WELL

Top 10 Vintage Tips

1. Prohibit young people from travel

No young person under forty is ever to be allowed to travel abroad under any circumstances; nor is anyone to be allowed to go for private reasons, but only on some public business, as a herald or ambassador or as an observer of one sort or another.

Plato, *Republic* (*c.*380BCE)

2. Avoid foreign novelties, customs, and affections

In manners or behaviour, your Lordship must not be caught with novelty, which is pleasing to young men; nor infected with custom, which makes us keep our own ill graces, and participate of those we see every day; nor given to affection (a general fault of most of our English travellers), which is both displeasing and ridiculous.

Francis Bacon, *Essays* (1597)

3. Consider the monsters

Have you considered all the dangers of so great an enterprise, the costs, the difficulty, the expectation, the conclusion, and everything else pertinent, and weighed them properly in your judgement? There is heaven, you say, but perhaps you can scarcely see it through the continuous darkness. There is earth, which you won't dare to tread upon perhaps, because of the multitude of beasts and serpents. There are men, but you would prefer to do without their company. What if some Patagonian Polyphemus [Cyclops] were to tear you to pieces and then straightaway devour the throbbing and still-living parts?

Joseph Hall, *Another World and Yet the Same* (1605)

4. Prohibit fools, furious people, and women from travel

It may be doubted whether all persons may...undertake Travel...Infants and decrepit persons...fooles, madde men and furious persons whose disabilities of mind are such as no hope can be expected for the one or other. Lastly, the Sex in most Countries prohibiteth women, who are rather for the house than the field.

Thomas 'the Travailer' Palmer, *An Essay of the Means how to make our Trauailes, into forraine Countries, the more profitable and honourable* (1606)

5. Map the universe

It were of use to inform himself (before he undertakes his Voyage,) by the best Chorographical and Geographical Map of the Situation of the country he goes to, both in it self and Relatively to the Universe.

Edward Leigh, *Three Diatribes* (1671)

6. Adopt local fashions and avoid being eaten

All Persons that travel in *Turky* must change their Habit into that of the Country, and must lay aside the Hat and wear a Turbant, and the meaner the Habit the safer they will be from Extortions and Robberies...The best Mony they can carry are *Spanish* Pieces of Eight, provided they be full weight, and not of Peru...

It is absolutely necessary to carry good Arms to defend themselves upon all occasions, but more particularly to fight the *Arabs,* and other Rovers. Above all, it is requisite in *Turky* that Travellers be arm'd with Patience to bear many Affronts the Infidels will put upon them, and with Prudence and Moderation to prevent, as much as possibly may be, any such Insolences... When they travel with the Caravan, they must take care never to be far from it, for fear of being devour'd by wild Beasts, or by the wilder *Arabs.*

Anon, "The History of Navigation" in *A Collection of Voyages and Travels* (1704)

7. Fear not death

A young man is good constitution, who is bound on an enterprise sanctioned by experienced travellers, does not run very great risks. Let those who doubt, refer to the history of the various expeditions encouraged by the Royal Geographical Society, and they will see how few deaths have occurred... Savages rarely murder newcomers.

Francis Galton, *The Art of Travel* (1855)

8. Pack sensibly for train journeys, and remember ladies need more time

- Divide your luggage into packages, and attach to the inner side of the lid of each package a list of the various articles which such package contains; then number each package, and finally make a memorandum of these lots, with their corresponding numbers, in your pocket-book.

- Label your luggage legibly, and boldly. Observe, also, that the name of the place should be in larger letters than the name of the person; and however much this may offend our self-esteem, it must be borne in mind that in the hurry and bustle of departure, the destination is what is first required to be known, the owner being a secondary consideration.

- Be on time: trains wait for no man. And, should there be ladies in the case, it is absolutely necessary to allow a wider margin for the preparations for departure than is ordinary assigned. The fair sex *must* complete their toilet to their entire satisfaction, whatever the consequences may be. It should also be remembered that they do not enter into the spirit of the straight-laced punctuality observed by the railway authorities, and if the time-table sets down the departure at 1.20, they instinctively read 1.45.

Anon, The Railway Traveller's Handy Book (1862)

9. Avoid hurrying and worrying

- The American who visits Europe for the first time is apt to be in a hurry, and to endeavour to see too much. He will very likely return with a confused notion of his experiences, and will be obliged to refer to his note-book to know what he has done. Instances have occurred of tourists who could not tell whether St. Paul's Cathedral was in London or Rome, and who had a vague impression that the tomb of Napoleon was beneath the Arc de Triomphe.

- do not disturb yourself with unpleasant thoughts of what may happen in the fog. Remember, rather, that of the thousands of voyages that have been made across the Atlantic only a few dozens have been unfortunate, and of all the steamers that have plowed these waters only the *President, City of Glasgow, Pacific, Tempest, United Kingdom, City of Boston, and Ismailia* - seven in all—are unheard from. The chances are thousands to one in your favor.

- In regions where there are highwayman, facetiously termed 'road agents' by the Californians, carry as little money as possible, and leave your valuable gold watch behind... Generally the first intimation of their presence is the profusion of several rifles or pistoles into the windows of the coach, with a request, more or less polite, for you to hand over your valuables. When you have no alternative but to hand over, do so with alacrity, and lead your assailants to think it the happiest moment of your life.

Thomas W. Knox, *How to Travel: Hints, Advice, and Suggestions to Travelers by Land and Sea all over the Globe* (1881)

10. On trains, beware hats and ham sandwiches

- Deerstalker caps are affected by many women in travelling, but suit very few.
- Avoid pastry as you would the plague...sandwiches may be eaten, provided they are not of ham.
- Tea at the refreshment-rooms of railway stations and on board steam-boats is often a mere parody on the real article—a fearful decoction.

Lillias Campbell Davidson, *Hints to Lady Travellers* (1889)

1

WHY DO PHILOSOPHERS CARE ABOUT TRAVEL?

> The supreme moments of travel are born of beauty
> and strangeness.
>
> Robert Byron, *First Russia, Then Tibet* (1933)

The train wasn't crowded but its passengers were loud. Two seats behind me, a couple were quarrelling over Trump and Hillary. Two seats ahead, a couple were noisily engaging in a sex act.

This prompted a hushed debate across the aisle.

'She has her *face* in his *pants*.'

'Well, dear, all the more reason not to talk to her.'

The whispers dragged my gaze to the window again.

It was early spring, ice break-up season in Alaska. Fingers of sleet slushed across the glass, blurring trees into snow and blotting out hills. I'd boarded the *Aurora Winter* in Anchorage, the state's biggest city, and was now headed inland to Fairbanks. My journey would take all day but most passengers were onboard for a few hours, or less. Some flagged down the train from one snowdrift only to hop off at a seemingly identical snowdrift twenty minutes later. I peered past the drifts into forests, and imagined leafy trails leading to log cabins.

Returning to my book, I tried to ignore the groans and grumbling rising around me. They do say that travel broadens the mind.

There's a myth that philosophers don't travel. It is fuelled by Socrates, who never set foot outside the city walls of Athens; and by Kant, who never travelled more than a hundred miles from his birthplace of Königsberg. What's more, the 'philosophy of travel' is not a recognized field of enquiry. There are no books on the philosophy of travel, no university lecture courses, no conferences.

Despite all this, many philosophers care about travel. The notion of a 'travelling philosopher' is ancient. Strabo, geographer and traveller writing at the turn of the first century, included those 'looking for the meaning of life' among those addicted to 'mountain roaming'. 'The wisest heroes were those who visited many places,' Strabo said, 'for the poets regard it as a great achievement to have seen the cities and know the minds of men'.[1]

Some philosophers travelled extensively. Confucius spent years travelling through states now part of China, and legend has it that his contemporary Laozi wrote most of his teachings at a border crossing. Descartes fought as a soldier in Eastern Europe and later became something of a vagabond. Thomas Hobbes, Margaret Cavendish, and John Locke wandered the European continent in political exile. In the twentieth century, W. V. Quine used steamers and aeroplanes to visit 137 countries, and Simone de Beauvoir used her trip to China to write a book.

Philosophers have also argued travel is important. Francis Bacon claimed travel would bring about the apocalypse— in a good way. Jean-Jacques Rousseau thought it was essential to education. Henry Thoreau believed we would all be happier if we ventured into the wilderness and picked huckleberries.

Travel is tangled with philosophy. It poses philosophical questions. Can meeting unfamiliar peoples tell us anything about human minds? Is it ethical to visit the Great Barrier Reef if its corals are withering? Is travel all about men? Further, philosophy has affected travel. The philosophy of space encouraged seaside tourism. Philosophical ideas about the sublime spurred mountain climbing and caving. Philosophy of science produced travelling scientists like John Ray and Charles Darwin, and encouraged every sailor on the high seas to collect far-flung rocks, plants, and cryptic objects 'of strange operation'.

The philosophy of travel isn't a thing, but it should be. Asking questions about travel, and exploring ways philosophy has changed travel, can help us think more deeply about our journeys. Thinking more deeply about things is usually worthwhile: it can increase our appreciation and enjoyment of them. Along the way, this expedition will show that not all philosophers are as hidebound as you might think—many led lives beyond the armchair. George Berkeley fought off wolves in a French mountain pass. Isaac Barrow battled pirates whilst sailing to Turkey (although he loses gangster points for later describing this skirmish in Latin verse).

Why do philosophers care about travel? The sixteenth-century French philosopher Michel de Montaigne offers an answer. Montaigne spent years roaming Switzerland, Germany, and Italy, and his 1580 *Essays* are riddled with reflections on travel.[2] He argues travel shows us the diversity and variety of the world, forcing the soul to continually observe 'new and unknown things'. Travel shows us *otherness*.

We experience otherness when we come into contact with the unfamiliar—it is the feeling that things are different, alien. My favourite travel books describe far-flung places. Sara Wheeler's *Terra Incognita* explores Antarctica. Paul Theroux's *Great Railway Bazaar* encompasses Europe, the Middle East, and Asia. Eric Newby's *A Short Walk in the Hindu Kush* describes trekking through Afghanistan. These tales convey a strong sense of otherness. Wheeler writes that, in Antarctica, her points of reference dissolved, like the volcanic plumes of Erebus. Theroux describes a bowl of soup, containing whiskers and bits of intestine 'cut to look like macaroni'. Quoting from a Bashgali phrase book, Newby reveals the harshness of daily life in the Afghan mountains: 'I saw a corpse in a field this morning.' 'I have nine fingers; you have ten.' 'A dwarf has come to ask for food.'

Otherness can explain the distinctions we draw between journeys. All journeys involve motion, change of place over time. Little motions fill our lives. We move from bedrooms to kitchens, we drive to see friends, we walk dogs around parks. Yet when we speak of 'going travelling', we are thinking in grander terms: we are thinking of journeys such as Wheeler's or Newby's. What's the difference between a trip to the grocery store, and a trip to the Sahara? Why is a drive to visit family different from driving through Botswana?

The difference between everyday journeys and travel journeys is not a matter of distance. Many travel journeys involve long distances—Wheeler, Theroux, and Newby all travelled thousands of miles. Yet travel in the grander sense doesn't always involve such distance. Samuel Johnson travelled just a few hundred miles to write his *Journey to the Western Islands of Scotland*, and Bill Bryson's *Lost Continent* starts in his hometown. It is also possible to undertake lengthy journeys that are not travel journeys. In Jules Verne's novel *Around the World in Eighty Days*, Phileas Fogg circles the globe, yet tries to avoid experiencing the countries he passes through, 'being one of those Englishmen who are wont to see foreign countries through the eyes of their domestics'. More mundanely, imagine a lawyer flying from London to Hong Kong, sitting through some meetings, and flying back again. Her journey would have covered almost 6,000 miles—yet it seems to be an everyday journey, not a travel journey.

I think the difference between everyday journeys and travel journeys lies in how much otherness the traveller experiences. Everyday journeys involve just a little, whereas travel journeys involve a lot. Travel writers often aim to increase their experience of the unfamiliar. In a 1950 interview, Swiss adventurer Ella Maillart explains she prefers to travel alone because any companion becomes 'a detached piece of Europe'. Their reactions will be European, and that will restrict her to a European frame of mind—together they build a foreign cell. 'I want to forget my western outlook,' Maillart said, 'feel the whole impact made on me by the newness I meet at every step'.[3] Today, many travellers recommend 'old school' travel, going abroad without mobile phones or laptops.[4] Technology can cocoon us, wrapping us in familiar weather apps and social media. One motivation for travelling off grid is to avoid insulating yourself from the new.

When and where do people feel otherness? That depends on who we are. Human beings each possess a unique set of memories, desires, beliefs. Language, food, or architecture that is familiar to one person may not be familiar to another. This is why travel books are as much about their writers as their places. If a glaciologist lived in Antarctica and wrote a travelogue about it, she would end up with a very different book to Wheeler's *Terra Incognita*. Her experience would have been different, because what was *different* to her would have been different.

Montaigne repeatedly reminds his readers that what is new to one person is, to another, daily habit. Promiscuity. Patricide. Infanticide. Some societies condemn these practices, whilst other societies allow them. Montaigne argues against 'exoticizing' unfamiliar peoples, against making them appear too different from familiar ones. In an essay 'On Cannibals' Montaigne discusses a group of people from Brazil who reportedly practised cannibalism. He argues this practise is not as strange as it first appears, for historically European soldiers have eaten corpses during famines. There is no harm in 'making use' of our dead carcasses, and it is far less 'barbarous' than the French art of torture. Montaigne goes on to describe the landscape the people live in, their houses, dances, marriages, and gods. These aspects of their lives would have seemed familiar to Montaigne's readers— their own lives involve dancing, marrying, and worship. Montaigne's conclusion about this far-flung people is sardonic. 'All this does not sound very ill, but then, forsooth, they wear no breeches.'

Travel can be good for us because otherness is good for us. Montaigne tells us that travel is beneficial: it teaches the advantages of bathing, and conjugal friendships are 'warmed by absence'. Even better, experiencing the other improves our minds. Considering new and unfamiliar things forces us to expand and rethink what we know. As traveller James Howell put in 1642, the fruits of Forreine Travell include 'delightful ideas, and a thousand various thoughts'.[5]

René Descartes agrees that it's useful to experience the unfamiliar. He writes it is good to know something of the customs of various peoples, so we do not think everything contrary to our own ways is 'ridiculous and irrational'.[6] Customs are conventional ways of behaving. For example, the British often eat chips with mushy peas. In contrast, the Dutch often eat chips with mayonnaise. Strange though both habits are, neither is ridiculous nor irrational. Travel shows us that our own customs may not be the best; it forces us to question what we take to be obvious.

The twentieth-century philosopher Bertrand Russell also argued that travel is good for us, and that living abroad diminishes prejudice. However, Russell drolly warns against elevating all foreign customs:

> In the seventeenth century, when the Manchus conquered China, it was the custom among the Chinese for the women to have small feet, and among the Manchus for the men to wear pigtails. Instead of each dropping their own foolish custom, they each adopted the foolish custom of the other, and the Chinese continued to wear pigtails until they shook off the dominion of the Manchus in the revolution of 1911.[7]

Travel and cultural exchange is desirable, but we must always be wary of pigtails.

Several philosophers compared their enquiries to journeys, and I think they're aiming at the same idea. Berkeley likened one of his investigations to a 'long Voyage', involving difficult travel across 'wild Mazes of Philosophy'. Halfway through his *Treatise of Human Nature*, David Hume reflects on the trip he has already taken, and on what is yet to come. 'Methinks I am like a man, who having struck on many shoals, and having narrowly escap'd ship-wreck ... has yet the temerity to put out to sea in the same leaky weather-beaten vessel.' He is tempted to remain on his current 'barren rock', rather than venture out onto 'that boundless ocean, which runs out into immensity'. Just like travellers, through their philosophies Berkeley and Hume are cutting new paths in the wilderness. They are setting off into the unknown—the unfamiliar—but they implicitly think the rewards are worth it. They are broadening their minds, seeking out new truths. Berkeley proudly describes his philosophical conclusions as a homecoming. Hume the sceptic is less pleased with himself, although he adds that when his philosophical speculations become too cold and strained, he can always make merry with friends, and play a game of backgammon.[8]

Unfortunately, I suspect it was easier in Montaigne's lifetime to undertake travel journeys than it is today. That's because many of the processes designed to make travel easier in the twenty-first century also reduce otherness. To explain this, let's look at an argument from historian Paul Fussell.

In his groundbreaking book *Abroad*, Fussell harangues tourism. Fussell argues travel is different to tourism. Travel occurred during the eighteenth, nineteenth, and early twentieth centuries. It fused the 'unpredictable' excitement of exploration with the pleasurable tourist sensation of 'knowing where one is'. According to Fussell, there is no travel left—only tourism. Fussell traces its roots to the mid-nineteenth century, 'when Thomas Cook got the bright idea of shipping sightseeing groups to the Continent'. Tourists seek things that have been 'discovered by entrepreneurship', and prepared 'by the arts of mass publicity'. Fussell points towards tourist institutions like Butlin's holiday camps, or French 'Club Med' vacation villages 'where nudity and pop-beads replace clothes and cash'.[9]

Fussell published his travel–tourist distinction in the 1980s, and it has many problems. If Fussell is right, then most 'travellers' were European, wealthy, white, and male.[10] No matter how far or how long someone travels for in the twenty-first century, they will never be a 'traveller'.

Although I don't think Fussell was right about that, he was on to something. I share Fussell's intuition that, for a European, journeying to a French vacation village is less *travel* than, say, Maillart's trip to Beijing via the Taklamakan desert. That difference lies in otherness. Holiday packages and tourist villages muffle the unfamiliar. You don't handle booking websites in foreign languages; you don't read local signposts to figure out where you're going. You can hang out with holidaymakers from your own country. Order familiar meals in a familiar language. Travel is about the experience of otherness, and some tourist mechanisms get in the way of that.

Since Montaigne's day, the world itself has been transformed. Travel writers often lament impending 'global homogenization', the world becoming everywhere the same. Bill Bryson describes Anywhere, USA. 'Placeless places that sprout up along the junctions of interstate highways—purplishly-lit islands of motels, gas stations, shopping centres and fast food.'[11] These outcrops can be found all over the world, usually filled with the same mushrooms: Best Western, Shell, McDonalds, KFC.

Yet complaints about homogenization have a longer history than you might think. 'All capitals are just alike', moaned Rousseau in the eighteenth century, 'Paris and London seem to me the same town'. In the nineteenth, John Stuart Mill entertained similar worries: Europe is losing its 'remarkable diversity of character and culture', and 'making all people alike'.[12]

If the world is homogenizing, it will be harder to experience new things whilst travelling. But it is far from impossible. The trick is simply to get away from what you know. For the Western traveller, that means getting out of formica airports, avoiding Irish pubs and Starbucks, engaging directly with people and places. As Maillart writes, you can feel as brave as explorers starting for the unknown, the first time you address a 'witty' taxi-driver in Paris, or risk climbing down into a Tibetan pub for a meal 'smelling of rotten meat'.[13] It might be harder for us to find otherness but it is definitely still out there.

My own journey into the unfamiliar began in Groningen, a city in the northernmost Netherlands. It's so far to the north that, in winter, night falls at three o'clock. I had lived there for several years, and spent most of that time writing a history of seventeenth-century theories of time. The book had become far too familiar. It was mammoth, and difficult, and I had *finally* finished a full draft. I pressed 'send' on my email to the publisher then stumbled out into the dark.

I wandered canals and cobbled *straten*, peering into bright shops and cafes. I needed a break and began planning a holiday—somewhere utterly unlike quaint, chocolate-box pretty Groningen. In the Vismarkt I came across a stall selling cardboard sculptures. A silver moose stared down at me, its snout all planes and angles. Blue origami antlers spiked upwards. I decided to visit Alaska.

In the weeks that followed, researching my trip to the 49th State somehow became mixed up with the philosophy of travel. Before I quite understood what was happening, I was leaving the library with stacks of books. *How to Lie with Maps. The British and The Grand Tour. The Idea of Wilderness.* I crammed knowledge into my eyes with both hands. Soon my brain was stuffed with colourful yet useless facts, like a dusty box of Christmas ornaments. Descartes packed 2,000 books on his last, fateful voyage to Sweden. Victorian women explorers had ulterior motives for travelling in skirts. Antarctic tourists forget everything they ever learn about penguins. And that was how I ended up in the Land of the Midnight Sun, reading Montaigne.

The train journey to Fairbanks was advertised as majestic, and it was. The carriages rumbled through sugar-crusted forests, past lakes dotted with caribou. One length of track spindled out over Hurricane Gulch, a bridge arching three hundred feet up. I hung out of the window, woolly hat rammed over my ears, and gazed at the monochrome world of rock and spruce unfurling below.

Despite its beauty, for most of the passengers this train ride was ordinary, familiar. They were visiting relatives in Wasilla, or commuting to Talkeetna, or shopping. I was one of the few striking out into unknown territory, travelling into polar Trump country. What is other to one person is not to another.

Eventually, the sex noise culprits retreated to the toilet. Meanwhile, the political commentators found common ground in their disgust over Bernie Sanders:

'He's a *socialist*.'

We were all travelling the same route through space, yet making different journeys.

2

WHAT ARE MAPS?

Brian Harley on Cartographic Deception

I power-walked down Fifth Avenue, breath huffing, hands jammed into pockets. I'd flown in from Amsterdam the previous night and jet lag clutched at me. The conference had started that morning but the talks on Spinoza and vacuums felt unreal, hallucinatory. I was trying to throw it all off by getting outside. New York smells hung in the air. Baking bread. Pepperoni. Garbage. A fragile March sun appeared, gilding the pavements. I gazed upwards through zigzagging fire escapes. Pigeons cooed where the sky flared blue.

Using Google, I found a second-hand bookshop. Bells tinkled above the door, the only bright thing about the place. I found a sales clerk and asked about maps.

'Wrap—wrapping paper?' His face screwed up. 'We don't sell that here.'

'Ah, no,' I said, in my troublesome British accent.

After a quick chat about *Harry Potter* I was free to explore the maps section. Edging between bookshelves into a gloomy alcove, I stepped carefully to avoid spilling papers over the floor. Orange Ordnance Surveys overhung their shelf. Rows of atlases formed uneven teeth. Kneeling down,

I hunted through ranks of red Rand McNallys. I would arrive in Anchorage two weeks from now, and I wanted to make plans. At the very end of a row, I found an *Alaska State Map*. I smoothed its accordion folds flat, the paper rippling over my shoes.

Once unfolded, the map lit up the space. Islands and coastal ridges edged against the sea. The landscape glowed white and green, delicately veined with roads and rivers. The Yukon River branched across the paper, dots traced the Alaskan oil pipeline. Livengood, Deadhorse, Moose Creek, Coldfoot. The place names read as though the map-maker had enjoyed adventures.

Maps are all around us, all the time. I had rarely spared their nature a thought. What is a map? My yellowing copy of James Monteith's *First Lessons in Geography* defines a map as 'A picture of the whole, or a part, of the Earth's Surface'.[1]

Before I began research, that sounded about right—the description fit my Google map of Manhattan. Sure, maps don't have to be *pictures* in the traditional sense. You can build a map out of clay, or weave it into a tapestry. You can tattoo a map onto your body (world map tattoos[2] were a trend in 2016). Nor do maps have to depict the *Earth's surface*. Maps can depict things above and below us: weather systems, underground metros, oil reservoirs. Maps can also depict things beyond the Earth: moons, stars, black holes. If Monteith wanted to be more precise, maybe he should have said that a map is a 'visual representation' of 'any part of reality'. But, I thought, he was basically there.

That was my thinking until I began reading about the philosophy of maps. The word 'map' comes from the Latin *mappa*, meaning a white cloth, like a flat tablecloth. Humans were making maps before they made Latin. The oldest surviving world map was painted around 8,000 years ago on a cave wall at Jaora in Madhya Pradesh, India. Until the twentieth century, people defined maps in largely the same way Monteith had.[3] On this definition, maps are 'transparent', they are what they appear to be: representations of reality.

This doesn't mean that maps must be complete, or accurate. Historical maps are neither. In the first century, Plutarch complained about geographers filling the margins of their maps, such that beyond the known world lies only 'sandy deserts full of wild beasts, unapproachable bogs, Scythian ice, or a frozen sea'.

Look at these maps in Figure 2.1 from Thomas Burnet's 1684 *Theory of the Earth*.

Burnet labelled large portions of these maps *incognita*, unknown. Today, we label them Washington State, Canada, Antarctica. The maps are wildly inaccurate. Most of Australia is missing. The map-maker has sliced an island off the western edge of the United States. Eighteenth-century maps contained so many inaccuracies that travellers were advised to carry compasses and note down where maps were faulty.[4] As human science and technology has improved, so has the accuracy of our maps. Satellite imaging represents our planet with never-before-seen accuracy. We can be confident we are not missing any major land masses.

I have always held the transparent view of maps. Atlases? Just a kind of book. Country maps? Helpful for planning overland treks. City maps? Useful to find museums. I was convinced otherwise by Brian Harley's 1989 article, 'Deconstructing the Map'. Harley used philosophy to show us the dark side of maps.

'Metaphysics' is the branch of philosophy that investigates reality. It asks: What is real? What could be real? What are real things like? Metaphysics usually studies the things

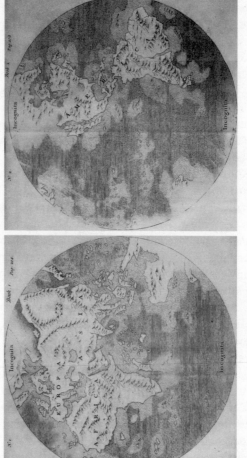

Figure 2.1 *Burnet's Theory of the Earth*

around us: atoms, material bodies, our minds. Yet we can turn metaphysics on anything, and Harley turned it onto maps. He argued we can break maps down into parts and show that, far from being straightforward, maps are complex and opaque. They are objects of influence and power. Metaphysically, maps are deceptive.

Harley provided two lines of argument. First, Harley showed that maps are 'rhetoric' devices: maps are seeking to persuade or influence their readers. Throughout history, map-makers have placed their homeland at the centre of their world maps. Harley argues that what is, and what is not, centred in a map is a rhetorical choice. Centring Athens or Jerusalem on a map adds a subtext of 'geopolitical force' to what appears to be a straightforward representation of the planet.

Similarly, consider what maps do and do not represent. Take my *Netherlands* road atlas. This map highlights castles and churches, while townhouses are inconspicuous. It traces the boundaries around country estates, and ignores boundaries between farms. The map achieves this by enlarging some symbols and shrinking others, rendering some place-names in bold and others in italic. Some lines are dotted, others are thick and colourful. Harley argued that maps embody rules of 'social order'. In the map-maker's society, it is 'taken for granted' that a castle is more important than a peasant's house. A gentleman's estate is more significant than a farmer's. This means that a map-maker is not just recording the shape of the physical and human landscape—they are also recording the contours of feudalism or social class.[5]

We can illustrate Harley's point using world maps.[6] In 1569, the Flemish map-maker Geradus Mercator developed the 'Mercator' world map; see Figure 2.2. It places Western Europe firmly in the centre. Although the Mercator map is

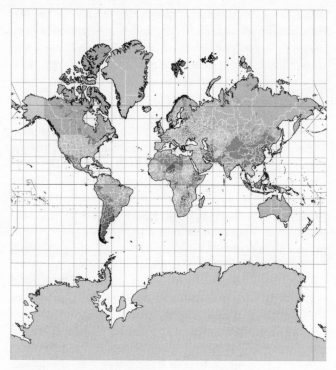

Figure 2.2 *A Mercator map*

used in schools, it is inaccurate in various ways. Africa and Australia are shrunk, and Antarctica dominates the whole.

The 'Authagraph' map, recently produced by Japanese map-makers, aims to correct these inaccuracies; see Figure 2.3.

In the process, it also moves Japan closer to the centre.

If you type 'American world map' into Google images, you'll see plenty of world maps placing the United States at the centre. Similarly, Chinese world maps centre on China. In 2006, the Norwegian foreign minister funded a new

Figure 2.3 *An Authagraph map*

set of maps, centring on the 'High North': Norway and the surrounding polar regions. In a speech, the minister explained that the High North should no longer be seen as 'a cold and desolate wilderness'. It is an important place in Europe, an emerging 'energy province'.[7] The Norwegian minister is aiming to place Norway at the centre of the map in more ways than one.

What maps represent matters. Take borders. Some maps place Tibet inside China. Some draw the Palestine–Israel border far away from Jerusalem. Other maps parcel Kashmir with Pakistan. Researchers have investigated the placement of borders alongside disputed territories on Google Maps. They have shown that the location of these borders jumps, depending on your web servers' location. For example, on Russian servers, Google Maps shows disputed territory in Crimea as Russian rather than Ukrainian.[8] Less dramatically, the United Kingdom is redrawing the borders of political constituencies. Although this is supposed to be a response to shifting population demographics, critics have suggested the government is trying to win political advantage over its opposition.[9]

Having shown that maps seek to influence people, Harley moved on to his second line of argument. Maps embody power. Map-making has been funded by monarchs, governments, and churches to further their own ends. Britain's national mapping agency is called the 'Ordnance Survey'. This is an odd name, as 'ordnance' usually refers to military supplies. The explanation lies in the origins of the Ordnance Survey, which stretches back to the 1740s. An English duke, 'Butcher' Cumberland, decided that mapping the Scottish Highlands was essential in defeating Scottish rebels.

Maps contain knowledge and so, like enemy intelligence, they were often guarded. Harley points to a 1988 *New York*

Times article, 'Soviet Aide Admits Maps Were Faked for 50 Years'.[10] It describes how public Russian maps were deliberately falsified. Rivers and streets were misplaced, boundaries distorted, and geographical features omitted. (The US army noticed these errors, and made a list of towns that 'peregrinated'—wandered in puzzling ways.) In 2016, the CIA released a huge batch of recently declassified maps, showing Moscow, divided Berlin, Baghdad, and Cuba. Maps embody knowledge and power.

Harley has provided us with an alternative metaphysics of maps. On Harley's 'opaque' account of maps, maps are *not* representations of reality. Instead, maps are packets of information, produced by humans to communicate with other humans. These communications seek to persuade their readers. *This* part of the world is a military or intellectual centre, a country has *these* borders, oil deposits are *here*. Rather than representing reality, maps may seek to create it.

Were all the maps in this world destroyed and vanished under the direction of some malevolent hand, each man would be blind again, each city be made a stranger to the next, each landmark become a meaningless signpost pointing to nothing.

Yet, looking at it, feeling it, running a finger along its lines, it is a cold thing, a map, humourless and dull, born of calipers and a draughtsman's board. That coastline there, that ragged scraw of scarlet ink, shows neither sand nor sea nor rock; it speaks of no mariner, blundering full sail in wakeless seas, to bequeath, on sheepskin or a slab of wood, a priceless scribble to posterity. This brown blot that marks a mountain has, for the casual eye, no other significance, though twenty men, or ten, or only one, may have squandered life to climb it.

Beryl Markham, *West with the Night* (1942)

And that's not all that's strange about maps. More recently, people have challenged the idea that maps are outside the mind. Whilst investigating the metaphysics of a thing, you might ask: Does its existence depend on minds? If you are a *realist* about something, you think it exists independently of minds. I am a realist about trees, mountains, and stars. If a virus eradicated conscious beings from Earth, I believe these things would continue to exist.

In contrast, if you are an *idealist* about something, you think its existence depends on minds. You can hold idealism about all kinds of things. Some philosophers of mind are idealists about emotion. They think that, if there were no minds, there couldn't be sadness or happiness. Some philosophers of perception are idealists about colour. They think colour is a mental quirk of conscious beings, and in reality the world merely contains light rays and particles. Blues and greens and yellows exist only in our heads.

Should we be realists or idealists about maps? You might think we should obviously be realists about maps. They are solid objects we can hold in our hands, not thoughts or perceptions. However, Rob Kitchin and Martin Dodge have recently argued maps only *become* maps when they are read. An unread map is merely a 'set of points, lines and colours...ink on a page'. They claim this page only becomes a map when it is read or interpreted, 'made to do work in the world'.[11] Only then are its points and lines decoded, set in a human context, and given meaning. You might think the same is true of a book. Without anybody to read it, a copy of *Pride and Prejudice* is just ink printed on wafers of tree pulp.

If Kitchin and Dodge are right, maps are mind-*de*pendent things. If maps depend on being read, and only human minds can read, then maps depend on human minds. We should be idealists about them. If humans died out, we would leave behind scrawled papers but no maps.

Here's a last strange thing about maps. They may not be *things* at all. Consider online maps. We don't know when the first map was made but we do know when the most recent one was created: a fraction of a second ago. The world wide web was invented in 1989, the same year Harley published his article. (I dimly remember life before the web, although none of my students do.) The internet revolutionized cartography. Before its invention, maps depended on paper and printing technology. Maps were expensive to make and to buy. Today, we can make and use maps for free, a process which takes map-making power away from monarchs and governments and puts it into public hands.[12] Experts estimate over two hundred million online maps are distributed daily—that's more than are printed on paper in the whole world.[13]

Online maps are not only free, they are *processual*. Metaphysics distinguishes between 'things' and 'processes'. Things include chairs, kettles, vases. Things are static, unchanging. In contrast, processes include rivers and thunderstorms. A storm isn't static, it is continually unfolding and changing.

Are maps things or processes? We usually think of maps as things: the maps in these pages lie inert. Yet online maps do not remain still. Google Maps and Apple Maps and OpenStreetMap are constantly changing, updated from minute to minute. We could think of online maps as things with a very short lifespan. Each time Google Maps is updated, a new map comes into being. The next time Google Maps is updated, the old map ceases to exist, and a new one emerges in its place. If this were true, then each Google Map exists for just a few seconds, however long the gap between updates lasts.

The problem with conceiving Google Maps as continually creating and destroying maps is that it doesn't fit with our experience of using the programme. It doesn't *feel* as though maps are continually coming in and out of existence. Rather, it feels as though there is one map that is continually changing, through its updates. Perhaps we are better off conceiving Google Maps as processes. Online maps have more in common with thunderstorms or rivers, than with chairs and kettles.

Some older maps seem closer to processes too. In the British Library I once saw a wartime map of central London. The map's original lines were partly obscured by paper rectangles, meticulously layered and glued. As bombers destroyed London's streets, people deleted them on the map. J. R. R. Tolkien's maps of Middle Earth grew in a similar way. As Tolkien's thinking progressed, he glued new sections of map over older parts.[14]

Strange creatures though they are, I take great pleasure in maps, and I am far from the only person to do so. Back in 1589, the geographer Thomas Blundeville remarked, many 'delight to looke on Mappes'—although he adds that many do not understand them.[15]

Many writers have taken maps as subjects. In her poem 'The Map', Elizabeth Bishop playfully muddles Nova Scotia's towns with the maps depicting them. (Bishop also finds beauty in Monteith's stark geographical lessons, and uses them in her work.) Sharon Olds' 'Topography' describes the bodies of two lovers as maps.[16] Today, you can buy whimsical maps showing whisky distilleries in Scotland, and maps of fairy homes in Iceland. You might worry that Harley's view of maps as doom-laden objects of power overlooks this whimsy. Take Tolkien's maps of Mordor. They portray a place called Mount Doom but they are far from doom-laden. There can be a lighter side to map-making.[17]

Philosophy has convinced me that maps belie their simple appearance. As Figure 2.4, the very first lesson of Monteith's *Lessons in Geography*, explains:

This is a picture of the WORLD or EARTH upon which we
live. It is a GREAL BALL. The part you see is the outside or
surface, and is either land or water.

Figure 2.4 *Monteith's Lessons in Geography*

Elegant though Monteith's description is, it misses the map's petticoat complexity. Maps are like puff pastry: thinly and invisibly layered. I wonder if this partly accounts for the glamour of maps. We are often attracted to powerful things: people, cars, storms. Through their layers, maps can be just as powerful.

3

FRANCIS BACON ON THE PHILOSOPHY OF SCIENCE AND FROZEN CHICKEN

As I stepped off the train in Fairbanks, arctic air blasted my face. It tasted of tin. The daylight dwindling, the carriages gleamed dusk pink. I tried not to smile as the lusty couple pushed past me to nab a taxi. Shouldering my backpack, I said goodbyes to people I'd talked with on the journey. The blue-bobble-hat lady who had shared boiled eggs, whilst explaining how Obama had faked his birth certificate. The conductor who believed the government was turning the Northern Lights into weapons.

Having been squished in a seat all day, I decided to walk into Fairbanks. It was warm enough once I started out, although I didn't see another soul on the streets. The city's outskirts seemed poor and empty. Snow clung to the roofs and green spaces, the river was still frozen. Most of the buildings were squat cubes, huddling together. Presumably easier to heat. As I entered the leafier suburbs, clapboard houses popped up, all stripes and triangles. I was staying in one of them, an old-fashioned bed and breakfast advertising an Aga and clawfoot baths. The place was as corny as I'd hoped: overwrought American historic, full of gold twiddles and lace. Doilies had invaded.

I was the only person staying in the building—even the girl who checked me in didn't sleep there.

'This is shoulder season, tourist-wise', the girl explained. 'Too late for winter stuff but too early for summer stuff.'

'That's fine. Is there anything to do in the evenings?'

The girl winced and shot me the full 'stupid tourist' look. 'Right.'

I spent the evening writing. I sat in the parlour, which was large but felt cramped. A monster mahogany table dominated the space and mismatched display cases lined the walls, jutting out at odd angles. Chandeliers threw queer oblongs of light, hinting at gilt picture frames and silver teapots. The bulbs weren't bright enough to actually illuminate the room so the edges remained dark, lumpy shadows roosting in corners. My laptop glowed upwards, outlining what appeared to be a taxidermied musk ox. I wondered what early scientists would have made of it.

Western science owes a colossal debt to early modern thinker Francis Bacon. Once upon a time, Europeans believed we could understand plants and animals just by thinking about them. You could sit in an armchair and *reason* that mosses are a kind of plant, whilst lichens are an algae-fungi mix. At the turn of the seventeenth century, Bacon overturned that myth. He transformed European philosophy of science, arguing we can't understand the natural world just by thinking about it. And travel was central to Bacon's vision.

Bacon studied at Cambridge and travelled through France before starting a political career. His star waxed and waned throughout his lifetime. At its heights, Bacon served as a member of Parliament, as Queen's Council, as Lord Chancellor. At its lows, he was imprisoned for debt, and impeached for corruption. Over the course of his career, Bacon wrote on religion, ethics, law, society, philosophy, and science. He even found time to write part of a utopian novel, *New Atlantis*.

During Bacon's lifetime, 'science' as we know it did not exist. Philosophy did. At its broadest, philosophy is the study of reality, and our relationships with it. Today, philosophy includes all sorts of things, from metaphysics to ethics. Historically, philosophy was even broader—it also included 'natural philosophy'. The natural philosopher investigated the natural world, looking at the biology of plants and animals, the chemistry of strange liquids, the physics of moving bodies and planets.

Although natural philosophy sounds a lot like the science we know today, there are differences. Whilst studying birds and rocks, natural philosophers also investigated the immortality of human souls, and God's earthly workings. This is why early science is so tangled with philosophy and theology. Descartes' pioneering theory of ocean tides is grounded on his metaphysics of matter. Newton's theory of gravity, and its groundbreaking account of planetary movements, is rooted in God. Western science arguably emerged as an independent discipline in the nineteenth century: William Whewell coined the English word 'scientist' in 1833 (after noting that Mr Coleridge forbade gentlemen of science to describe themselves as 'philosophers').[1] Through philosophy of science, Bacon kickstarted the process by which science distinguished itself from philosophy.

Tables, birds, hills, rocks, stars: all these things comprise the material world we live in. As this world was traditionally investigated through reason, a medieval philosopher who wanted to understand oak trees would think about them. They might begin by pondering the nature of *matter*, then the nature of *living matter*, and work up to the nature of *trees*.

Bacon argued this medieval approach was foolish—he compared it to the way a spider's web is drawn out of the spider's own entrails. In place of this traditional approach, Bacon argued for 'experimentalism'. Experimentalists gather information about the world through observation and experiment. Bacon compared experimentalists to bumble-bees. They collect the products of nature, 'flowers of garden and field', and transform them into the honey of real knowledge.[2]

Bacon wasn't just interested in collecting scientific data. He was also interested in the philosophy underlying experimentalism. Slowly, Bacon developed a new philosophy of science. He argued we should collect information about the world through observation and experiment, and use that information to create axioms (principles). We would test axioms through more observation and experimentation, generating more general axioms.

You can picture Bacon's method as a kind of ladder. On the bottom rung, scientists collect information about particular things. For example, a biologist observing North American animals notices that many moose shed hair in May. Moving up the ladder, she formulates an axiom: 'Alaskan moose shed their winter coats in spring'. She could test this axiom through further observation. If the axiom seems sound, she could combine it with other axioms about moose. Another might be, 'Shiras moose shed their winter coats in spring.' Moving further up the ladder, the biologist could make a more general observation, '*All* moose shed their winter coats in spring.'

By collecting data and creating axioms about it, science would progress. Although Bacon stressed observation, and running experiments, he didn't seek to erase armchair thought altogether. Our world contains some things whose nature we can only understand by thinking—including science itself.

The next morning I took the bus to Fairbanks' Museum of the North. It's a striking building, all white ridges and curves. A cross between the Sydney Opera House and an iceberg. I spent an hour poking around the Gallery of Alaska, peering into display cases and reading dinky cards. The focus was on natural history: mastodon bones, gold and other mineral wonders, stuffed eagles, beavers, caribou. The 'Blue Babe' reigned over all, a mummified Ice Age steppe bison dug out of the permafrost.

I think Francis Bacon would have approved of this museum. His 1620 *The Great Instauration (Instauratio Magna)* argued that humans should create a complete natural history. The Museum of the North is working towards a small piece of this puzzle, providing a natural history of Alaska. Bacon was well aware that a natural history of the *universe* would be enormous—he described the project as 'royal', because it would require great labour and expense.[3]

The Great Instauration highlighted the following subjects for study:

- History of the Heavenly Bodies; or Astronomical History
- History of Lightnings, Thunderbolts, Thunders, and Coruscations
- History of Showers, Ordinary, Stormy, and Prodigious; also of Waterspouts (as they are called) and the like
- History of Clouds, as they are seen above
- History of Air as a whole, or in the Configuration of the World
- History of Hail, Snow, Frost, Hoar-frost, Fog, Dew, and the like
- History of Earth and Sea; of the Shape and Compass of them, and their Configurations compared with each other; and of

their broadening or narrowing; of Islands in the Sea; of Gulfs of the Sea, and Salt Lakes within the Land; Isthmuses and Promontories

- History of the Motions (if any be) of the Globe of Earth and Sea; and of the Experiments from which such motions may be collected

- History of Flame and of things Ignited

- Chemical History of Metals and Minerals

- History of Fishes, and the Parts and Generation of them

- History of Ebbs and Flows of the Sea; Currents, Undulations, and other Motions of the Sea

- History of the other Accidents of the Sea; its Saltness, its Various Colours, its Depth; also of Rocks, Mountains and Vallies under the Sea, and the like.[4]

Bacon was nothing if not ambitious. He even demanded a natural history of juggling.

Travel was key to this project. For Bacon, we cannot understand the seas and its fish by sitting in armchairs. People must go out into the world and look about. Figure 3.1, the frontispiece of *The Great Instauration*, emphasizes the importance of travel. One of its ships is sailing away into a boundless ocean, and the other is returning, riding low in the water because of the wealth it carries.

The ships sit between the Pillars of Hercules, the rocks flanking the Strait of Gibraltar. In Greek and Roman mythology, Hercules is the adventurous son of the god Zeus or Jupiter. In one myth, Hercules travelled as far as these pillars, and they came to represent the limits of the known world. The pillars were inscribed 'nothing more beyond' (*nec plus ultra*), a warning that ships should sail no further. (Mark Twain's *Innocents Abroad* complains that the ancients wrote book after book about the pillars but never mentioned

Figure 3.1 *Bacon's The Great Instauration*

the existence of the American continent: 'yet they must have known it was there'.)

In Bacon's frontispiece, the ships are sailing *beyond* the pillars. This symbolized Bacon's view that we should expand the limits of our knowledge. Beneath the ships, a line reads, 'Many shall go to and fro, and knowledge shall increase' (*Multi pertransibunt et augebitur scientia*). Travel will swell our understanding of the world.

Bacon's requests were well timed. Europe was experiencing its 'Age of Discovery', a slice of Western history running from the late fifteenth century to the seventeenth. European shipbuilding and navigation techniques had progressed to the point where long voyages were reasonably safe, and ships set off to see what lay beyond the horizon. They searched for new trade routes, and new lands to colonize— careless of peoples who already lived there.

Portuguese, French, Spanish, Dutch, and British sailors led the charge. In the 1490s, Christopher Columbus sailed to the Americas, in a failed attempt to find the west coast of Asia. In 1500, Pedro Alvares Cabral sailed from India to Brazil, claiming Brazil for Portugal. Martin Frobisher explored Canada and attempted to find the elusive north- west passage: a suspected trade route for Europe to Asia via the Arctic Ocean. Around 1520, Ferdinand Magellan circumnavigated the globe. In 1578, Francis Drake reached the Pacific by becoming the first Englishman to navigate the newly named Straits of Magellan. In the 1660s and 1670s James Cook charted and claimed parts of Alaska, New Zealand, and Australia.

Europeans were stirred by these voyages. John Seller's 1670 British *Atlas Maritimus* proudly lists 'The Discoveries that have been made within this two hundred years, by the Worthies of our own Nation, as well as Strangers'.[5] Seller describes how Richard Chancellor found a sea passage to

Russia. Henry Hudson came to the latitude of 81 degrees in attempting to discover the North Pole, and discovered Hudson's Bay. Hugh Willoughby discovered Greenland, dubbed 'King James his New-Land', before he 'was frozen to death'.

Bacon clearly believed that, just as Columbus had gone beyond Europe, intellectuals should go beyond their medieval heritage. Later illustrations of the Pillars sometimes changed their inscription from 'nothing more beyond' to 'go farther still'.

Was it a coincidence that Bacon began lauding travel during the so-called Age of Discovery? Of course not. Just like Seller, Bacon was swept up in the tide that expanded the European world. And that helped me answer a question that had arisen in my research. Early on, I realized this book would only explore Western philosophy of travel. Future books would be needed to explore travel in Chinese, Indian, or African philosophy. (Although philosophies travel too, and Western philosophy is rooted in classical Greek philosophy which may in turn stem from African philosophy—Aristotle credits the Egyptians with many important ideas.[6]) Notwithstanding the odd remark from Plato, the oldest Western treatments of philosophy and travel I could find were in Montaigne, Bacon, and Descartes. Why was that? What happened during the sixteenth and seventeenth centuries to turn European philosophers towards travel? The answer, I realized, was the European Age of Discovery. Travel was becoming a huge part of European society, and the philosophers became just as involved as everyone else.

Bacon's ambition cannot be underestimated. Whilst European explorers aimed at creating world maps, Bacon literally aimed at creating a new world. Bacon did not merely believe his new philosophy of science would lead to a complete natural history. He also believed it would lead to the apocalypse.

Today, the word 'apocalypse' usually means the end of the world—in the worst way. It pops up in discussions of nuclear war, or radical climate change. In seventeenth-century Europe, the word also means the end of the world, but with the possibility of renewal. Like most people of his period, Bacon believed humans had fallen from divine grace but they would be restored to it. The book of Genesis describes 'the Fall' of humankind. God created Adam and Eve in a paradise, the Garden of Eden. A serpent tempts Eve into eating a forbidden apple, Eve persuades Adam to eat too, and God expels them from Eden. Later, the Bible writes that God will eventually restore humans to paradise, 'making all things new'. Passages such as Revelation 21:1–5 mention the renewal of Jerusalem, so this city may be at the centre of the new paradise. At the centre of Jerusalem is the Temple of Solomon, which will be rebuilt.

You may have puzzled at the title of Bacon's *Great Instauration*. The archaic word 'instauration' means renewal or restoration, and it is particularly connected with the rebuilding of Solomon's Temple. Bacon dedicated his *Great Instauration* to King James I, who was known as the 'new Solomon'. So, Bacon is telling his readers that his new scientific method will ultimately restore Solomon's Temple, and humans to paradise.

Once you've seen a few religious symbols in Bacon's work, you see them everywhere. Let's return to the frontispiece of *Great Instauration*. The line below the ships is taken from a biblical prophecy on what will precede the apocalypse:

And there shall be a time of trouble, such as never has been since there was a nation till that time...And many of those

> who sleep in the dust of the earth shall awake, some to ever-lasting life, and some to shame and everlasting contempt. And those who are wise shall shine like the brightness of the sky above...Many shall go to and fro, and knowledge shall increase (Daniel 12:1–4).

Increasing travel and knowledge is a sign the end of the world is coming, but in a good way.

Bacon was well aware of the symbolization he introduced, writing elsewhere:

> It would disgrace us, now that the wide spaces of the material globe, the lands and seas, have been broached and explored, if the limits of the intellectual globe should be set by the narrow discoveries of the ancients. Nor are those two enterprises, the opening up of the earth and the opening up of the new sciences, linked and yoked together in any trivial way. Distant voyages and travels have brought to light many things in nature, which may throw fresh light on human philosophy and science and correct by experience the opinions and conjectures of the ancients. Not only reason but prophecy connects the two. What else can the prophet mean who, in speaking about the last times, says, Many will pass through and knowledge will be multiplied? Does he not imply that the passing through or perambulation of the round earth and the increase or multiplication of science were destined to the same age and century?[7]

This prophecy supports the connection Bacon draws between travel and science.[8]

Bacon underscored the importance of going out into the world throughout his life, and this eventually killed him. According to one account of his final days, Bacon was travelling by coach through Highgate when he leapt out into an unseasonable snowfall. He knew that meat could be preserved with salt, and wanted to test if cold would also work. Bacon bought a hen from a poor woman, 'made the woman gut it', and then stuffed it himself with snow. Carrying the chicken back into the coach, perhaps even riding with the icy bird on his lap, he caught a fatal chill.

From his deathbed, Bacon wrote to a friend:

> I was likely to have had the fortune of Caius Plinius the elder, who lost his life by trying an experiment about the burning of Mount Vesuvius. For I was also desirous to try an experiment or two touching the conservation and indur-ation of bodies. As for the experiment itself, it succeeded excellently well.[9]

Bacon had discovered frozen chicken. And, in a bizarre twist, the chicken's ghost is said to haunt Pond Square—the spot where it died. The half-plucked spectre was seen for centuries, with Air Raid Wardens reporting several sightings during the Second World War.[10]

After his death, Bacon's philosophy of science galvanized scientific research. It started a chain of events that led, amongst other things, to the natural history museums we know today. His influence peaked during the mid-seventeenth century, when a group of natural philosophers inspired by Bacon established the British Royal Society. Led by the likes of Robert Hooke and Robert Boyle, they aimed to carry through the Baconian vision of a complete natural history.

Like Bacon, the Royal Society were fixated on gathering data about far-flung lands. They met to discuss the latest travel books, and travel 'curiosities'—such as the latest packet of plant seeds. Its members published their findings in their very own periodical, *Philosophical Transactions of the Royal Society*. This is often credited as the first scientific journal.

Although the Society's work thrived, it was sometimes derailed by drunkenness. In 1664, the fellows set up a special committee to read travel literature. They drew up a list of books, and each member picked a book from the list to peruse. However, one fellow later explained in a letter that, instead of reading, they retired to their host's wine cellar. 'I leave you to guesse what our coresspondence and entertainment was under ground, in the Grotto, and neer the well, that is the Conservatory of so many dozen of wine bottles.'

In addition to reading (or attempting to read) new travel books, the Royal Society began publishing requests for information. Robert Boyle, the founding father of chemistry, authored one of these requests, titled *General Heads for a Natural History of a Countrey, Great or small.* Boyle requested the following kinds of information about foreign countries:

- the Longitude and Latitude of the Place
- the Temperature of the Air
- What Meteors the air is most or least wont to breed
- what kinds of fish are to be found in the Country: their Store, Bigness, Goodness, Seasons, Haunts, Peculiarities of any kind.[11]

Similarly, Edward Leigh asks after a country's climate, the 'goodness or barrenness of the Ground', the populousness of the people, its commodities, herbs, beasts, birds, fishes, and insects.[12]

The Royal Society's new understanding of travel as data collection affected European travel in many ways. First, it led to a new kind of traveller: the scientist. To make this point, let's look at a 1606 taxonomy of travellers, created by an English knight.

Sir Thomas 'The Travailer' Palmer focuses on 'regular' travel, 'an honourable or honest action of men'. Palmer does not explain what he means by 'irregular' travel, although he writes darkly 'most men finde by experience what it is'. Palmer distinguishes three kinds of regular travellers. *Involuntary* travellers did not choose to be abroad, they have been banished or exiled. *Non-voluntary* travellers are abroad to conduct state business: peacekeepers, ambassadors, 'men of warre', and spies. (Helpfully, Palmer advises spies, 'To keep themselves from being known for Intelligencers'.) *Voluntary* travellers have chosen to go abroad, to advance their own interests: mercenaries, traders, students, and doctors.[13] The kind of traveller that is wholly missing from Palmer's taxonomy is the natural philosopher, or scientist. The idea of such a traveller didn't exist at the start of the seventeenth century, but thanks to the Royal Society it did exist by the end.

Early travelling scientists included Henry Blount, John Ray, and Francis Willughby. In the nineteenth century, Charles Darwin continued this tradition through his *Beagle* expedition. Darwin actually opens *The Origin of Species* with a quote from Bacon, stating that no man can 'search too far or be too well studied' in divinity or philosophy.[14]

Many other kinds of travellers also contributed to the Royal Society's project: navy captains, colonial governors, ambassadors, merchants. Their help was especially welcome to the Royal Society because it was *free*, their salaries paid by other sources.

The second effect the Royal Society had on travel concerned travel destinations. From the 1660s, the Society began asking for information on specific places, including Greenland, the Caribbean, Hungary, Transylvania, Africa, Egypt, Persia, Virginia, and Brazil. Fellows gleaned information about these places from travel books, but what scanty information they had often led to further questions:

- 'Whether there be such little dwarfish men in the vaults of the Canaries, as was reported'?
- Is there a place in Brazil where 'that wood is, which attracts fishes, and of the fish, which turns to the wind, when suspended by a thread'?

- in Brazil, can toads be created by 'throwing a kind of Moorish Water'?
- Whether in Egypt, 'the appearance of the legs and arms of men appearing out of the ground, to a very great number, at a place five miles from the city of Cairo on good Friday, do still continue? and how that imposture is performed?'
- Of Iceland, 'What is said there concerning raining mice?'[15]

The connection between travel and science has persisted throughout British exploration history. Take the race to the South Pole. Many English-language histories claim Amundsen was 'only' interested in reaching the Pole, whilst Scott is lauded for his equal interest in Antarctic research.

The third effect was that a mania for curiosities developed. Scientifically minded travellers began flooding the Royal Society with artefacts. In 1704, one European rejoiced:

> Natural and Moral History is embellished with the most beneficial Increase of so many thousands of Plants it had never before received, so many Drugs and Spices, such variety of Beasts, Birds and Fishes, such varieties in Minerals, Mountains and Waters, such unaccountable diversity of Climates and Men.[16]

The stranger these artefacts were, the better.

That's because, on Bacon's philosophy of science, rare things are important. Rare things might be natural or handcrafted: elephants or newfangled pendulum clocks. Bacon also believed we should study 'monsters'. Collecting information about abnormal biological creatures, such as two-headed goats, would improve our understanding of nature's workings. Collections of such strange objects became known as 'cabinets of curiosity'.

In the mid-seventeenth century, Robert Hubert amassed a hoard of such things, described in *A Catalogue of the many natural Rarities, with great Industry, Cost, and Thirty Years Travel into foreign Parts*. His cabinet contained 'Whole Fishes' and 'Parts of Fishes', an Egyptian mummy 'adorned with hieroglyphics', 'Stones of Strange shape', a piece of 'old worms-eaten barke of a tree in stone', a Syrian giant's bone, a 'rose of Jericho, that is an hundred years old', and other 'Things of strange Operation'. The scientist and architect Robert Hooke bought Hubert's collection for the Royal Society. The idea of a natural history museum was born.

'Curiosities' were not always inanimate. Explorers brought home living plants and animals, including cacti and tigers. Horrifically, explorers sometimes took home *humans*. Christopher Columbus returned to Spain with seven Indians. Brazilian natives were showcased in French royal pageants. Frobisher exhibited an Eskimo. These people rarely survived for long. Sometimes they were submitted to further indignities after death, their bodies put on display for public viewing.[17]

Finally, the Royal Society affected travel writing. In various pieces, Bacon raged against flowery language. *The Great Instauration* tells us to do away with 'ornaments of speech, similitudes, treasury of eloquence, and such like emptinesses'. Instead, he urged travellers to write 'briefly and concisely'.[18] In a 1669 book of essays, Boyle explains he has tried to write in a 'philosophical' strain. He desires his writing to be 'clear and significant', rather than 'curiously adorned'. He compares using 'needless rhetorical ornaments' to painting the eye of a telescope.[19]

Pretty though it might be to paint the lens of a telescope, it would not help us to see the stars. The idea was that reports must be clear *and* trustworthy. Bacon preaches caution about what we admit into our natural history. For example, authors must state whether they have observed a thing first-hand, or whether they are recording a second-hand description. If a report is second-hand, they must state whether it was made by a 'vain-speaking and light person' or one who is 'sober and severe'.[20]

The Royal Society desired clear and credible writing because, often, travel books were neither. Marco Polo's *c*.1300 *Travels* describes the 'ugly' unicorns that inhabit Java. John Mandeville's 1356 *Travels* describes the rib of a giant 'forty foot long', and explains that Natumeran islanders 'have heads like dogs'. (Despite their shape, Mandeville assures us these islanders are 'fully reasonable and intelligent'.)

The Royal Society's effect on Western travel writing was profound. The descriptive, scientific style it proscribed is found in James Cook's *Voyages*, Darwin's *Voyage of the Beagle*, and Cherry-Garrard's *Worst Journey in the World*. Taken to extremes, it injects science into what might otherwise be spiritual moments. One eighteenth-century traveller wrote of a mountain:

> We could not withdraw our eyes on the summit of the peak, from beholding the colour of the azure vault of the sky. Its intensity at the zenith appeared to correspond to 41 degrees of the cyanometer.[21]

Later travel writers sometimes apologized for violating these norms. Philosopher Mary Wollstonecraft does so in the preface to her 1796 *Letters Written During a Short Residence in Sweden, Norway and Denmark*. Wollstonecraft explains she could not avoid writing these letters in the first person, becoming the 'little hero' of each tale—although 'I tried to correct this fault'. This is not to say that Wollstonecraft abandoned the Society's style entirely.

Along the way, her *Letters* provide information on religious practices, mineral deposits, salt mining, and the possible existence of sea monsters.[22]

Bacon's philosophy of science is behind the importance that seventeenth-century natural philosophers attached to travel. Travel became central to early modern science, and it remains central today. In 2009, explorers in Vietnam opened up one of the world's largest underground caves. It contains an underground forest, and scientists are studying its 'new' organisms and plants.[23] The same year, geologists mapped Antarctica's under-snow mountains, and found them to be higher than the Alps.[24] In 2014, first contact was made with another tribe living in the Amazon rainforests. Anthropologists estimate many more such peoples remain.[25]

In the future, we will travel further underneath the seas, which remain a liquid mystery: we've currently mapped less than 0.05 per cent of the ocean floor.[26] This should further please Bacon, who asked after underwater mountains and valleys. We will also travel deeper into outer space, bringing back knowledge of distant star systems. When we do, we will go even farther than Bacon envisaged.

4

INNATE IDEAS IN DESCARTES, LOCKE, AND CANNIBALS

The People at the *Caribes*, Bay of *Soldania*, *Peru* and *Mengrelia* may be as good Men as the best-natured People in Europe, notwithstanding their awkward Customs in Cookery, and then eating of their own Children.

Henry Lee, *Anti-Scepticism* (1702)

The salesman at the car hire desk craned over me, keys in hand. 'Are you *sure* you'll be all right on the road?'

'Absolutely.'

We were around the same age, but he looked as though he was fighting an urge to pat me on the head. 'All right then. Come with me.'

We walked out to the car together and inspected the body for dents. Rainclouds were clumping overhead, so it was a quick inspection. As I signed the last form, clipboard balanced on the bonnet, the man nodded at the map on top of my bag. Various places north of Fairbanks were circled in pencil. 'Why do you want to go up there?' he asked.

I thought about the map's white spaces and the intriguingly named Deadhorse.

'It's hard to explain.'

Alaska is vast. It covers over 600,000 square miles—
that's about the same size as Mongolia. There are nearly
34,000 miles of shoreline and over 3 million lakes. It is
the largest American state, purchased by the United States
in 1867 for around two cents an acre. It wasn't sold by
native Alaskans, but by the Russian Empire.[1] Alaska's size
may explain why James Michener chose to start his 1988
novel about the place a billion years before the present day.
Alaska details its geological formation, its ice ages, the movements of 'adventurous dinosaurs', and the fish that would
one day evolve into salmon. Michener seemed to need that
remote perspective to put the land in view. The state's size
also goes some way to explaining its lack of infrastructure.
Many Alaskan communities remain unconnected to each
other by road, including Juneau, the state capital.

That said, Alaska has one big, famous road: the Dalton
Highway. Had the Romans made it as far as Alaska, they
would have recognized the determination that went into
building it. For long stretches at a time the 414-mile road
runs ruler straight, cutting Alaska in half, dipping down into
valleys and popping up again horizontal on the other side.
Made famous by the History Channel's *Ice Road Truckers*, the
road is a testament to what humans can do when they want
something badly enough: as part of the effort to construct
Alaska's oil pipeline, workers built it in five months. The road
was completed in 1974 and fully opened to the public in
1994. To label it 'remote' would be a clonking understatement:
the highway and its pipe run through acres and acres of
tundra wilderness. The 2016 Dalton Highway guide describe
the road as 'Mars Lite' because, in winter, temperatures can
drop to –60°C. Literally as cold as the Red Planet.

As I drove north up the Dalton, the flat, green landscape
grew frostier and bumpy. Snow clung to the ground and

spruce trees cradled snowballs twenty inches across. I passed clumps of blackened trees, charred by forest fire, sticks stark against the snow. Other vehicles were rare but the pipeline kept me company, dipping and climbing with the road, gleaming silver in the sun. Eventually I reached the Yukon River, the blue squiggle on my map transforming into a colossal gully of water. Turning off the highway, I parked beside a waist-high snowdrift. I found myself grinning—this was the Yukon. I put on wellies and plodded through the snow towards the shore.

Rounding the bend, I entered a world of white. The banks, the tundra, the water itself: all alabaster, shining. The only colour lay in the heart of the river, where thawing ice bled inky rivulets, green water puddling into mirrors.

One of my favourite childhood books is set on the Yukon. Velma Wallis's *Two Old Women* tells an Alaskan survival story. Sa' is 75 years old, and Ch'idzigyaak is 80 years old, yet these women snare squirrels and rabbits, trek using home-made snowshoes, gather spruce boughs for their beds, and carry live coals for fires. Despite the cold and their arthritic joints, these ladies make a cosy camp for themselves beside a river. Wallis is a native Alaskan of Gwich'in descent, and in the preface she explains how she heard this story from her mother, sitting where the Ts'it Han (Porcupine River) flows into the Han Gwachon (Yukon River).

Like Wallis's two old women, I was the only human about for tens of miles. I seemed to be the only thinking thing in this scenery, the only conscious being amongst the hoar-frost. If any animals were around, they were well hidden.

Consider how strange minds are. They seem to be quite unlike other things we share the world with. A rock cannot feel happy or sad. Although a rock can be cold, the rock cannot *feel* its coldness. Computers process information but they don't (yet) feel: a computer can record the colour of the sky but doesn't *see* the blue. Unlike rocks and computers, human minds have ideas: thoughts, beliefs, mental impressions of things. I have ideas about my car, the Eiffel Tower, and Denali Mountain. I have more complex ideas about Harry Potter, God, ethics. Since Plato, philosophers have wondered about the *origins* of our ideas. Do we start life without any ideas in our heads, and acquire them as we experience the world? Or are we born with some 'innate' ideas inside our heads already? In the seventeenth century, travel became snarled in these debates.

Historically, philosophers thought many of our ideas are innate. Descartes plays a starring role in this tradition. He grew up in France but early on resolved to travel, impressed by Montaigne's belief that travel is 'a very improving thing'.[2] Looking back over his career, Descartes describes his dissatisfaction with his early education, and explains:

> That is why, as soon as I was old enough to emerge from the control of my teachers, I entirely abandoned the study of letters. Resolving to seek no knowledge other than that which could be found in myself or else in the great book of the world, I spent the rest of my youth travelling, visiting courts and armies, mixing with people of diverse temperaments and ranks, gathering various experiences, testing myself in the situations which fortune offered me, and at all times reflecting upon whatever came my way so as to derive some profit from it.[3]

In 1618 he moved to the city of Breda (in today's Netherlands) where he studied mathematics and mechanics. This began a decade of travelling, through Germany, France, Italy, Denmark, and Hungary. Although Descartes claimed his travels were purposeful, biographer Desmond Clarke suggests he was just drifting.[4]

Eventually tiring, Descartes picked a country to settle in. He chose the Netherlands—the country apparently best suited to his temperament. Although Descartes had picked a country, he could not pick a city. Descartes continued travelling throughout the Netherlands, never staying in one place for more than a few months. By the end of this period, Descartes had lived in over a dozen Dutch cities, as illustrated in Figure 4.1.[5] One of Descartes' friends observed he suffered from 'wanderlust'. Descartes stayed in the

Figure 4.1 *Where Descartes lived*

Netherlands until 1649, when he accepted an invitation from Queen Christina of Sweden. Descartes was to bolster the intellectual community in Stockholm, and tutor Christina on philosophy. The trip did not go well. Christina met with Descartes infrequently, and then at library sessions starting at five o'clock in the morning. In a letter to his friend, fellow philosopher Elisabeth of Bohemia, Descartes wrote 'it seems to me as if men's thoughts freeze here during the winter in addition to the water'. He died in Stockholm, certainly of flu and likely of pneumonia.

Descartes' travels helped him to become open minded:

> In my college days I discovered that nothing can be imagined which is too strange or incredible to have been said by some philosopher; and since then I have recognized through my travels that those with a view quite contrary to ours are not on that account barbarians or savages, but that many of them make use of reason as much or more than we do.[6]

And he became a philosopher who questioned *everything*. Descartes' 1641 *Meditations* asked the following questions of its readers:

Is it possible you are insane?
Are you sure you're not dreaming right now?
Might you be hallucinating the world around you?

Descartes was trying to establish what we *really* know about the world. If you think it's possible that you're dreaming right now, then it is possible you are not where you think you are, nor are you actually reading this book. I believed I was standing by the Yukon, yet I could be asleep in Groningen. Perhaps I was hallucinating the snow and the ice. Perhaps I am an old woman dreaming I am younger.

Descartes' technique of doubting things we take to be true has become known as 'Cartesian scepticism'. It's a lethal technique, because once you've started it's difficult to stop. Every piece of knowledge humans take themselves to have can be doubted.

Every piece of knowledge, Descartes believed, except one. Descartes argues we can't doubt that we exist. Descartes reasons that as long as he is doubting, he exists—he is a thing, that doubts. This underlies the slogan, 'I think, therefore I am'. Even if you doubt you are reading this book, because you may be dreaming or hallucinating, you cannot doubt you are thinking and existing.

The problem is, if you think your existence is the *only* piece of knowledge you can be certain of, you don't know very much at all. I know that I exist, but I don't know that I am really standing beside a river, or have cold feet. Descartes' solution to this problem was to wheel in, quite literally, a *deus ex machina*. When Descartes looks inside himself, he finds various ideas, and one is an idea of God. For Descartes, this is the idea of a being that is 'infinite, independent, supremely intelligent, supremely powerful, and which created both myself and everything else'. Descartes asks where his ideas come from, and reasons that while many of our ideas come from experience, our idea of God must be innate. His idea of God is so perfect it *must* have been placed within him by a perfect being: by God himself.[7] Ultimately, Descartes uses the existence of God to stop doubting: he claims we can be sure we're not dreaming or hallucinating, because a perfect God would not allow us to be deceived.

Descartes' influence on Western philosophy was immense; he is sometimes described as the father of modern philosophy. After Descartes, many people came to agree that our idea of God is innate. There seemed to be no gainsaying him.

Until British philosopher John Locke came along. Born a few generations after Descartes, Locke studied at Oxford, where he became involved with many of the scientists who would later form the Royal Society. For his medical work, Locke himself was later elected a fellow. Like Descartes, Locke travelled widely through Europe, and his writings show a sense of humour.

For example, in a letter drafted in 1676, Locke details a horseback ride to the French city of Poix:

> & though that way of travelling tires an Englishman suffi-
> ciently, yet we were no sooner got into our chambers but we
> thought were come there too soon, for the highway seemed
> the much sweeter, cleaner and more desirable place.[8]

Locke goes on to describe how he asked his hosts for a pair of slippers, but was sent 'sturdy timber' clogs. Later, his hosts served the travellers 'a supper of ill meat & worse cookery'. Happily, Locke writes that after dinner the 'strong perfume' of his bedroom 'made me quite forget my slippers & supper'. He would not have lasted the night if not for a 'large, convenient hole in the wall' which provided plenty of fresh air.

Locke's journals also reveal his interest in science. At the Palace of Versailles, Locke notes the complex arrangement of fountains in a garden, and that the menagerie contained an elephant. Locke doesn't spend many words describing this 'vast mountain' of an animal but he is engrossed by its diet: 50 pounds of bread per day and 16 pounds of wine with rice.

Locke later returned to the European continent to escape political persecution. Locke had become close friends with Lord Anthony Ashley Cooper, first earl of Shaftsbury, a political giant whose star rose and fell whilst Britain figured out what kind of monarchy or parliament (if any) it wanted. Shaftsbury eventually fled to Holland, dying there in 1683. Locke crossed to the Netherlands the same year, and began travelling the country whilst writing philosophy. In 1688 the political winds shifted again, and it was safe for Locke to return to Britain. Once home, Locke began publishing enormous amounts of work, including his 1690 *An Essay Concerning Human Understanding*. As its title implies, the *Essay* asks how humans acquire knowledge. The first chapter gives Locke's aim: 'To inquire into the original, certainty, and extent of human knowledge, together with the grounds and degrees of belief, opinion, and assent'.[9] Although this is a philosophical project, Locke believed travel had a huge role to play in it.

Locke's own travels never took him beyond the bounds of Europe. Nonetheless, he was fascinated by travel that did go further. Locke interviewed returning travellers, and sent information requests to people abroad. For example, like Bacon, Locke was keen to get to the bottom of juggling. In a 1683 letter to a traveller friend about India, Locke explains that he has heard 'strange stories of the tricks done by some of their jugglers there'. Their feats seem to go beyond sleight of hand, and not to be within the power of art or nature, and Locke asks whether these jugglers are really as strange as reported. He is also keen to know whether Indians 'have any apparitions amongst them, and what thoughts of spirits', and for as much information as possible on the 'opinions, religion, and ceremonies of the Hindoos and other heathens of those countries'. Almost as an afterthought, Locke asks how the peoples of the East keep time, 'as months and years'.[10] Locke's friends obliged him with information from their travels, and also sent him travel curiosities which he passed on to the Royal Society, such as seeds and bones.

Locke's library held maps, geographical surveys, and nearly two hundred travel books.[11] Locke took notes on many of these books, and commissioned watercolour copies of their sketches. He was especially interested in illustrations of native peoples. Locke advised Awnsham Churchill on editing his *Collection of Voyages and Travels.* Locke may even have authored its anonymous essay, 'The History of Navigation'.[12] This essay lists the advantages of travel: it has improved our knowledge of the globe, shown that no parts of the Earth are uninhabitable 'unless the dozen Polar Regions', given new constellations to astronomy, raised trade to the highest pitch, and extended the 'Empire of *Europe*' to the utmost bounds of the Earth.[13] Back then, many people were proud of Empire building, heedless of the harm it caused.

It might seem that Locke was an omnivorous reader of travel books. However, historian Ann Talbot has argued that Locke's reading was not as indiscriminate as it appears. In fact, Locke's travel books were chosen carefully: they focus on human social behaviour. Locke was actually attempting to study human behaviour as Francis Bacon might have done.[14] To explain this, let's return to the Baconian method of science.

Bacon believed we should study the natural world through observation and experiment. Usually, these techniques were *only* applied to landscapes, animals, and plants. Unlike animals and plants, humans were believed to be 'above' the natural world. This is because humans have immaterial souls, specially created by God. Consequently, humans were still studied using theology or philosophy.

If you applied Bacon's techniques to humans, you were declaring that humans are part of the natural world. This suggests humans may lack souls, and hints at denying their creator: God. During this period, Europe condemned atheists. Women (and a few men) were executed for witchcraft. The Roman Inquisition imprisoned Galileo for maintaining, contrary to Christian belief, that the Earth moves around the sun. Spinoza was persecuted for his perceived atheism.

In this setting, it would be extremely controversial to include the study of humans within natural history. Nonetheless, Bacon did. His *Great Instauration* asks for information on human bodies, which was socially acceptable:

- History of Humours in Man; Blood, Bile, Seed, &c
- History of Excrements; Spittle, Urine, Sweats, Stools, Hair of the Head, Hairs of the Body, Whitlows, Nails, and the like
- History of Sleep and Dreams
- History of Life and Death
- History Medicinal of Diseases, and the Symptoms and Signs of them

But it also asks for information on other aspects of humans, including:

- History of the Affections; as Anger, Love, Shame, &c.

Many people found this part of Bacon's project impossible to follow.[15] Robert Boyle did not.

Boyle instructs travellers to foreign parts:

> There must be a careful account given of the Inhabitants themselves, both Natives and Strangers, that have been long settled there: And in particular, there Stature, Shape, Colour, Features, Strength, Agility, Beauty (or the want of it) Complexions, Hair, Diet, Inclinations, and Customs that seem not due to Education.[16]

But Boyle's own interest lay in science. To illustrate, take Boyle's fascination with a report about weather magic.

An English ship became becalmed in the West Indies, and a Native American shaman conjured up a wind for it. The captain reported that the sorceress, an 'old Hag', employed charms and ceremonies, blew into a fruit shell, and caused the clear sky to become overcast. The 'very dark Clouds' produced 'Thunder, Lightning, & a brisk Storm both of Rain & Wind'. You might assume that Boyle's interest in this report lay in the magic. Against this, one scholar argues Boyle's interest was more in 'meteorology' rather than 'comparative religion'.[17]

Through his obsession with travel books, Locke seemed to be carrying through Bacon's programme as it applies to humans. Through observation and experiment, Locke was collecting data on *people*. He continued Bacon's project in ways nobody else had.[18]

Locke used travel information to support various philosophical positions. For example, he used descriptions of foreign plants and animals to explore problems in the way we classify biological creatures. Later, these problems drive Locke's view that we can't know the real essences of creatures.[19] Locke used travel books to explore different ways of setting up governments. For example, he argues a tyrannical government can lead to cannibalism. Locke also used travel books to question widespread philosophical beliefs, including belief in innate ideas.

Locke's *Essay* accepts that humans have innate wants: 'Nature, I confess, has put into man a desire for happiness and an aversion to misery'.[20] However, he denies that humans are born with any innate ideas. Locke reasons that if an idea is innate, everybody must have it. It wouldn't make sense for humans to be born with an innate idea, and yet not have it later in life. Consequently, Locke argues if some people lack an idea, that idea cannot be innate to humans. We can't see the ideas inside other peoples' minds, so Locke argues we must examine their actions. If someone holds a particular idea, their actions will show this.

Many philosophers have argued that human ethical ideas and principles are innate. Locke considers an example, 'Parents preserve and cherish their Children'. Locke argues this principle cannot be innate, because large groups of people do not hold it. Using his travel research, Locke argues there have been whole nations of civilized peoples who have exposed their children in fields, to 'perish by Want, or wild Beasts'. Sometimes children are placed in the same graves as their mothers, if they die in childbirth; and children have been 'dispatched' if an astrologer declares them to have 'unhappy Stars'. Locke reports that the Christian Mengrelians, a people in Georgia, 'bury their Children alive without scruple'. Further, Locke claimed, there are places where people eat their own children. In the Caribbean, the Caribs 'were wont to geld their Children, on purpose to fat and eat them', and a people in Peru 'were wont to fat and eat their Children they got on their female Captives, which they kept as Concubines for that Purpose'.

What is important to Locke is that these practices are not 'condemned or scrupled' in their societies. The travel books that he uses to support his claims are, wherever possible, recent rather than historical. He also preferred research backed up by multiple sources.

Many of Locke's examples, such as the Caribbean and Peru, concern far-flung places. Consequently, a critic might object that Locke is using exceptionally 'savage and barbarous Nations' to make his points. To forestall this, Locke points out that infanticide has occurred amongst 'civilized' people too. He claims the Greeks and Romans often exposed their infants, 'without pity or remorse'.

Locke considers many more moral ideas that are supposedly innate. We should nurse the sick. We should bury the dead. We should avoid extra-marital sex. Using travel, Locke argues these ideas are not innate either:

> In a Part of *Asia*, the Sick, when their Case comes to be thought desperate, are carried out and laid on the Earth, before they are dead, and left there, exposed to Wind and Weather, to perish without Assistance or Pity... The Virtues, whereby the *Tououpinambas* [the Tupinambá people of Brazil] believed their merited Paradise, were, Revenge, and eating abundance of their Enemies... The Saints, who are canonised amongst the *Turks*, lead Lives, which one cannot with Modesty relate.

Infanticide. Cannibalism. The immodest lives of Turkish saints. The examples Locke choses are extreme, perhaps designed to shock his readers. Europeans found reports of humans eating humans frightful and difficult to believe, yet Marco Polo described cannibalistic practices in detail, and later explorers apparently confirmed these early tales. Locke concludes there are no innate ideas about morality.

The various ceremonies practiced before these idols are so wicked and diabolical that it would be nothing less than an abomination to give an account of them in this book. The reader should, however, be informed that the idolatrous inhabitants of these islands, when they seize the person of an enemy who has not the means of effecting his ransom for money, invite to their house all their relations and friends. Putting their prisoner to death they cook and eat the body, in a convivial manner, asserting that human flesh surpasses every other in the excellence of its flavour.

Marco Polo, 'Of the Nature of the Many Idols Worshopped in Zipangu [Japan] and of the People Being Addicted to Eating Human Flesh', *The Travels of Marco Polo* (c.1300).

The same actions are abhorred in one place, and praised in another.

Locke would have welcomed Wallis's tale of Alaskan survival, fictional though it may be. A disturbing aspect of *Two Old Women* is how Sa' and Ch'idzigyaak come to be left alone in the wilderness. In the opening chapters we learn they belong to a tribe that is struggling to survive the long, dark winter. The women are elderly, no longer helping physically with the tribe's day-to-day tasks, and complaining about their lot. The leader decides to abandon them, and the implication is that these women have been left behind to die. They are a burden which must be sacrificed if the larger tribe is to survive.

This practice, the killing or abandoning to death of the elderly, is known as 'senicide'. Different cultures take different attitudes towards it. Historically, senicide was practised (rarely but occasionally) amongst Arctic peoples, and in Japan and Greece. It may still be practised today in parts of India.[21] Take the moral principle, 'We should preserve the elderly'. Locke would say that, like all the others, this principle cannot be innate because it is not held by all humans.

Having blasted the view that moral ideas and principles are innate, Locke goes on to deny that humans have an innate idea of God. If Descartes were right and humans were born with an idea of God, all humans would have this idea. Yet, as Locke points out, we don't.

Locke claims the existence of atheists is 'branded upon the Records of History'. Further, through travel, we have discovered 'whole Nations' amongst whom there is 'no Notion of a God'. Again, Locke supports this claim with travel writing. For example, a report on Brazil's Tupinambá people states, 'They have no so much as a Name for God...No Acknowledgment of any God, no Religion, no Worship'.

He adds that atheism occurs in 'more civilized' countries too, including China and Siam (now known as Thailand). Locke argues if everyone held an innate idea of God, philosophers wouldn't need to convince atheists of anything.[22]

Travel plays a large role in Locke's arguments against innate ideas. Locke's *Essay* goes on to argue all our ideas come from *perceiving* the world, or *reflecting* on ideas we already have. My ideas about cars and rivers come from perception. My ideas about politics and philosophy come from reflection on ideas I already have. For Locke, God exists, yet we do not have an innate idea of him.

It would be wonderful to know how Descartes would have replied to Locke's attack on innate ideas. Unfortunately, Descartes died before Locke published his *Essay*. Nonetheless, several philosophers attacked Locke's views on innate ideas. The attack made in 1697 by English theologian Edward Stillingfleet is especially provocative.

Stillingfleet was horrified by Locke's view we lack an innate idea of God, and attacked Locke's use of travel books. He argues Locke's examples are 'ill chosen', for two reasons. The first is that Locke has selected travel books by authors who were not sufficiently acquainted with the people or language of a country; or whose testimony has been contradicted by other travellers, who stayed longer in a country and understood it better.

Locke replied to Stillingfleet in 1699, and staunchly defended his travel reports. For example, Locke retorts he took his information about Soldania (part of South Africa) from 'an Ambassador from the King of *England* to the *Great Mogul*'.[23] Despite Locke's reply, there is some truth in Stillingfleet's critique. The travel writing Locke used *was* sometimes inaccurate. This is partly because early modern travel reports frequently embedded racist or nationalist attitudes—attitudes that were, of course, reflected in the philosophers reading them.[24]

Consequently, travellers and intellectuals often misunderstood the societies or languages they engaged with. For example, whilst it is true that nations like China and Thailand are not traditionally Christian, they nonetheless have long religious histories, prominently featuring Buddhism. Similarly, African religions have been misunderstood. John Mbiti argues African spirituality was overlooked *because* religion permeates all parts of African life, and there is no formal distinction between the religious and the non-religious: 'Wherever the African is, there is his religion.'[25] Further, whilst anthropologists have recorded ritual cannibalism in various peoples around the world, early modern reports were grossly exaggerated. The tales that reached the ears of Locke and his peers, of fearsome man-eaters from the Caribbean, Africa, Peru, and Georgia, were usually inflated or false.[26] Explorers had a tendency to 'exoticize' peoples they were unfamiliar with, rendering them 'other'. What could be more exotic than unknown tribes, combing rainforests in search of human flesh?

However, these inaccuracies do not help Stillingfleet's case. That is because these travel reports were not inaccurate on the key point. There are many places abroad where people do not have an idea of the *Christian* God.

This brings us to Stillingfleet's second reason to believe that the travel books Locke uses are ill chosen. Stillingfleet acknowledges there are atheist peoples abroad. He references the Cafres in Soldania, and the Caiguae of Paraquaria (Paraguay). However, Stillingfleet argues that these people are 'so strangely bereft of common Sense, that they can hardly be reckoned among Mankind'.[27] In other words, these people are not really *people*.

Appalling though it is, Stillingfleet was not alone in taking this attitude. In 1702, Henry Lee considers Locke's view that no ideas are held by all humans, or 'universally consented' to. In a passage seemingly designed to offend as many people as possible, Lee writes:

> But if any Man will bring Children or Idiots, such as are born and continue deaf and dumb, as Arguments against universal Consent, or Mad-men out of Bedlam, Monsters of Men out of the Indies and Africa, as disowning those Laws of Nature, I am … [un]able to confute them.[28]

Lee seems to be in agreement with Stillingfleet. The 'Monsters of Men' found in the East Indies or Africa are not really men. As human rights activist Richard B. Moore explained back in the 1970s, this attitude fed into European slave practices. For example, he argues that Christopher Columbus painted the Carib as voracious cannibals with an eye to justifying the wholesale enslavement of this indigenous people.[29] African philosophers have since tackled the notion that non-Western peoples are not really people at length, arguing that of course their humanity is second to none.[30]

It is to Locke's credit that he rejects the claim that foreign peoples are not people. In his reply to Stillingfleet, Locke warns, 'you go near denying those *Cafers* to be Men'.[31] Locke is effectively upholding their humanity. We cannot say some humans are people, but not all.

If Locke is right that humans have no innate ideas, one consequence is that humans lack an innate idea of God. If this is the case, Descartes' reliance on that innate idea cannot pull him out of doubting. I may be dreaming or hallucinating the Yukon.

Today, few philosophers believe that humans have innate ideas about God or morality. Yet that does not mean nothing is innate. Following Noam Chomsky, many people believe human language acquisition is innate.[32] You might also think all human brains are hardwired to think about 'basic' features of the world in particular ways. Colours, spatial perception, numbers. If I can perceive colour, doesn't my brain understand it the same way yours does?

The answers are surprising, and travel is still playing a role in generating them. For example, European languages like English, French, and German distinguish between green and blue. We take this linguistic distinction to mark a real difference in the world. Green and blue are different colours, right? Perhaps not. Linguists have found many languages do *not* distinguish between green and blue. These languages often use one word that covers green and blue (sometimes translated into English as 'grue').[33] This explains why some traffic lights in Japan run red, yellow, *blue*.[34]

Researchers have made other unexpected discoveries too. For example, Brazil's Pirahãs tribe has hardly any words associated with time. Even more surprising—the Pirahãs don't use numbers, or even have a concept of counting.[35] Other languages discuss space differently. Suppose you want to give someone directions to the nearest petrol station. You might say, 'Turn left at the end of the road, then left again, and you'll see the station coming up on your right'. These kinds of directions are *egocentric*: they depend on the positioning of ourselves. In contrast, you might say, 'Head north, then west, the station is on the north side'. These directions are *geographic*: they are fixed, independently of our bodies. In everyday life, Westerners continually use egocentric concepts of space. 'Put the glass beside you.' 'The exit is behind your car.' Yet the language Guugu Yimithirr, used by some indigenous Australians, doesn't use *any* egocentric coordinates.[36] This may mean they think about space differently.

I have ideas about God, and about ethics, but I don't believe they're innate. I do, however, find it tempting to believe that the way I think about colours or numbers is innate. Would my experience of the world change if I didn't count numbers, or perceive the sky as blue and leaves as green? One way to answer this might be to spend time living amongst peoples whose worldviews are different to mine. Descartes' claim that all humans are born with the same idea of God is false. Yet his claims about what travel can show are true: people with views contrary to ours are worth listening to.

5

WHY DID TOURISM START?

Sex, Education, and the Grand Tour

Having passed the Yukon I continued north, driving slowly up the steep hills known as the 'Roller Coaster'. Truckers have gifted other parts of the highway with similarly inspiring names, including 'Oh Shit Corner', 'Beaver Hill', and 'Gobblers Knob'.

A few hours later I stopped at Finger Mountain, a broad hill topped by a curve of granite. The gnarled digit itself wasn't much but the panorama was spectacular. Wind whined around rocks, almost visible in the clear air. It left a metallic taste on my tongue. The tundra stretched into the horizon, pocketed by hollows and crusted with glitter. Patches of green pierced the permafrost. Snow crystals bounced over my boots. I breathed deeply of winter and thought how fortunate I was to be a tourist.

People have travelled throughout human history. Just look at Alaska: its first inhabitants arrived 15,000 years ago. The Amerind, Na-Dene, and Eskimo-Aleut peoples likely followed herd animals across the Bering Land Bridge, which joined Alaska with Eurasia.[1] The bridge flooded around 10,000 years ago but Alaskans weren't entirely isolated.

Researchers have found obsidian and leaded-bronze artefacts there which are 800 to 4,000 years old, suggesting that Alaskans were trading with Siberians.[2] This far predates Russian and European visits in the eighteenth century.[3] And nor was this travel one-way. The Alaskan Thule travelled to Greenland, where they successfully battled Vikings.[4]

Although humans have been travelling for tens of thousands of years, the luxury of tourism is relatively new. Tourists *choose* to travel, voluntarily spending their leisure time abroad for pleasure. This kind of travel is very different to that of a priest making a pilgrimage, or a refugee fleeing war. Although Thomas Palmer's 1606 taxonomy of travellers includes 'voluntary' travellers such as mercenaries and students, there is no mention of tourists. That is because the Western idea of leisure travel did not yet exist.

Leisure travel came into its own in the mid seventeenth century. By this time, Europeans had been 'discovering' the world for a hundred and fifty years and Montaigne, Bacon, and Descartes had waxed lyrical about the importance of travel. Books about exploration, travel, and natural philosophy began percolating through the European consciousness. They especially fired the British imagination, fanned by a brace of new English-language travel books.

One was Thomas Coryate's 1611 *Crudities: Hastily gobled up in Five Moneth's Travels*. It describes Coryate's journey, much of it on foot, across Europe. The book contained lots of practical information on the countries travelled through, including their history, food, and exchange rates. Coryate's aim was to encourage travel across Europe.[5] Although he is little known today, Coryate was once nicknamed Furcifer (fork-bearer), for introducing the fork to England.[6]

I observed a custome in all those Italian Cities and Townes through the which I passed, that is not used in any other country that I saw in my travels, neither doe I thinke that any other nation of Christendome doth use it, but only Italy.

The Italian and also most strangers that are commorant in Italy, doe alwaies at their meales use a little forke when they cut their meat. For while with their knife which they hold in one hand they cut the meate out of the dish, they fasten their forke which they hold in their other hand upon the same dish, so that whatsoever he be that sitting in the company of any others at meale, should unadvisedly touch the dish of meate with his fingers from which all at the table doe cut, he will give occasion of offence unto the company, as having transgressed the lawes of good manners, in so much that for his error he shall be at the least brow-beaten, if not reprehended in wordes.

Thomas Coryate (1611) *Crudities.*

Others included Fynes Morison's 1617 *An Itinerary: Containing His Ten Years Travel Through the Twelve Dominions of Germany, Bohemia, Switzerland, Netherland, Denmark, Poland, Italy, Turkey, France, England, Scotland and Ireland.* Meanwhile, William Lithgow's 1632 *Rare Adventures & Painfull Peregrinations* described travels across Europe, the Middle East, and northern Africa.

Books like these began encouraging aristocrats, the only people wealthy enough to afford it, to travel around Europe. Although the elite of many countries travelled, it was predominantly a British craze.[7] The number of travellers surged after 1648, which saw the end of the Thirty Years' War in central Europe. (Not that Europe was peaceful after this date: 1672–8 saw the Dutch War, 1733–8 saw the War of Polish Succession, 1739–48 saw the British–Spanish

War of Jenkins' Ear, and 1756–63 saw the European-wide Seven Years War.) Palmer advises travellers to avoid countries 'engaged with civil, or expected wars'.

Slowly, the journeys of young British noblemen developed into the 'Grand Tour'. The label dates to Richard Lassels's 1670 *An Italian Voyage*. Lassels writes sternly that no man will understand European histories unless he has made the '*Grand Tour*' of France and Italy. Although Lassels is credited with introducing the term 'Grand Tour' into English it is worth noting that he may not consider it to be English: Lassels warns us he affects 'a world of exotick words not yet naturalised in England'. The phrase is French in origin, as illustrated by a 1702 English–French dictionary which translates 'They took a great Range (Ramble, or Jaunt)' into 'Ils ont fait un grand tour'.

Etymology aside, the tour usually lasted for two to three years, and the route became formulaic. Travellers would leave London and cross the English Channel to Paris. From there, they would journey to Geneva, Barcelona, Turin, Florence, Padua, and Venice. Rome was the heart of the trip, and tourists visited much the same places then as today: its Colosseum, Pantheon, St Peter's Basilica, Sistine Chapel, and Vatican museums. After Rome, the more adventurous traveller might go on to Greece or Egypt. Others would circle home, perhaps taking in Vienna, Dresden, Berlin, Heidelberg, or Amsterdam.

Grand Tourists were usually male, aged between sixteen and twenty-two. They were accompanied by an older tutor known as a 'bear-leader', who led his charges from one city to another like dancing bears on a leash. These tutors were usually unremarkable priests or university teachers. Occasionally, they were intellectuals of note. The philosophers Thomas Hobbes, John Locke, George Berkeley, and Adam Smith all acted as bear-leaders.

Why did Grand Tourists choose to travel? Was their tourism merely inspired by the heady mix of exploration and travel books drifting through the 1640s air? No. I found there were also simpler motivations: education and sex.

Ostensibly, Grand Tourists travelled to finish off their schooling. Francis Bacon's 1625 essay 'On Travel' describes travel as an education, and instructs young men to keep a diary of the things they will see abroad. He suggests travellers should observe the courts of princes, specially when they give audiences to ambassadors; and the courts of justice, while they sit and hear causes. They should visit churches, monasteries, monuments, the walls and fortifications of cities and towns, havens and harbours, antiquities and ruins, libraries, colleges, lectures, shipping and navies, city houses and gardens. Not to be forgotten, travellers should also scope out foreign armouries, arsenals, ammunition stores, warehouses, horse exercises, fencing bouts, and soldier training.[8] For Bacon, philosopher of science extraordinaire, all travel is about *data gathering*.

Bacon's remarks seem to have inspired Isaac Newton. In a 1669 letter written to a younger Cambridge fellow who was about to travel abroad, Newton advises:

1 to observe ye policy wealth & state affaires of nations so far as a solitary Traveller may conveniently doe.

2 Their impositions ypone all sorts of People Trades or commodities yt are remarkable.

3 Their Laws & Customes how far they differ from ours.

4 Their Trades & Arts wherein they excel or come short of us in England.

5 Such fortifications as you shall meet wth, their fashion strength & advantages for defence; & other such military affaires as are considerable.

6 The power & respect belonging to their degrees of nobility or Magistracy.

7 It will not bee time misspent to make a Catalogue of the names & excellencys of those men that are most wise learned or esteemed in any nation.

8 Observe ye Mechanisme & manner of guiding ships.

9 Observe the produces of nature in several places especially mines with ye circumstances of mining & of extracting metalls.[9]

One reason this letter is bizarre is its emphasis on *mining*. Another reason is that Newton himself never stepped outside England (in fact, most of the travel advice is plagiarized from someone else's manuscript). Newton seems to have realized how odd it would be for a man not of the world to be dispensing worldly advice, for the letter appears unsent.

Other thinkers saw educational travel as a way of turning boys into gentlemen. The preface to Thomas Nugent's 1749 *The Grand Tour* travel guide offers a few remarks on 'that noble and ancient custom' of travelling. Nugent writes that this custom aims to visibly enrich the mind with knowledge, rectify one's judgement, and compose one's outward manners. Ultimately, travel will form the 'complete gentleman'.[10]

This idea was championed by Jean-Jacques Rousseau, who travelled a great deal himself. He was born in Geneva but, as a young man in 1742, made his way to Paris to become a musician. Later, he lived in Venice, and began publishing philosophy. From 1756, Rousseau moved around the French countryside, staying with wealthy friends. Ultimately, the Paris authorities condemned his work as irreligious, and Rousseau went into exile. He moved from Switzerland to Germany to England, returning to France incognito in 1767. Rousseau died in Paris three years later, copying music for a living.

Travel is a central theme in Rousseau's 1762 *Emile, or Treatise on Education*. This philosophical novel follows the growth of a boy, Emile, from birth into adulthood. Emile's tutor aims to provide the boy with morality, self-worth, and proper manners. The tutor describes taking Emile travelling on horseback:

> We do not travel like couriers but like explorers. We do not merely consider the beginning and the end, but the space between. The journey itself is a delight. We do not travel sitting, dismally imprisoned, so to speak, in a tightly closed cage. We do not travel with the ease and comfort of ladies. We do not deprive ourselves of the fresh air, nor the sight of the things about us, nor the opportunity of examining them at our pleasure. Emile will never enter a post-chaise.[11]

In an essay 'On Travel' attached to the end of the book, Rousseau explains why travel is so important to education:

> Travelling accelerates the progress of nature, and completes the man for good or evil. When a man returns from travelling about the world, he is what he will be all his life; there are more who return bad than good, because there are more who start with an inclination towards evil. In the course of their travels, young people, ill-educated and ill-behaved, pick up all the vices of the nations among whom they have sojourned, and none of the virtues with which those vices are associated; but those who, happily for themselves, are well-born, those whose good disposition has been well cultivated, those who travel with a real desire to learn, all such return better and wiser than they went. Emile will travel in this fashion.[12]

Emile, with his well-cultivated 'good disposition', will grow well and wisely.

By 1776, using the Grand Tour to educate became so widespread that Scottish philosopher Adam Smith complained of young people being packed off to foreign countries—instead of to university. Smith had studied at Oxford and Glasgow, and earned a professorship at Glasgow.

Unlike Rousseau, he was not impressed by the effects travel produced upon the young. Smith writes that young men generally return home 'conceited' and 'unprincipled', having spent the past three or four years 'in the most frivolous dissipation'.[13]

By this flowery phrase, Smith means that young Grand Tourists are frittering their time away—in sensual pleasures. This brings us to the dark side of the Grand Tour. If education was the *official* reason to travel the continent, the unofficial one was debauchery. Unbridled drinking, gambling, and sex. These are likely the travel motivations Palmer describes as 'irregular'.

Lassels's advice to Grand Tourists[14] shows he is well aware of these dangers. Lassels writes that the traveller should aim 'at his Profit', not only at his pleasures. 'I have known many Englishmen, who for want of right aiming, have missed the white of Breeding, whole Heavens breadth.' Lassels is punning here. The 'white of Breeding' means being well-mannered, *and* virtuous with regard to sexual activity. Lassels continues:

> For some in travelling, aim at nothing but to get loose from their Parents, or Schoolmasters, and to have the fingering of a petty Allowance; and these Men, when they come into *France*, care for seeing no Court, but the Tennis-Court; delight in seeing no Balls but Tennis-Balls; and forsake any Company, to toss whole days together with a tattered *Marker* in the *Tripot* [betting house].

Spending money, gambling, and playing tennis (!) are all risky. Yet riskier still are women:

> Others desire to go into Italy, only because they hear there are fine Courtesans in Venice...these Men travel a whole month together to Venice, for a Nights Lodging with an impudent Woman. And thus by a false aiming at breeding

abroad, they return with those Diseases which hinder them from breeding at home.

Lassels describes irresponsible bear-leaders who have locked their pupils 'in a Chamber with a wanton Woman, and taken the Key away with them'. Of course, impudent and wanton women can be a great attraction to young men.

Such women were certainly attractive to James Boswell. The writer is known for his diaries about life in London, and his biography of Samuel Johnson. It is less well known, although also well recorded in his letters and diaries, that Boswell sought women everywhere.

For example, in a letter dated 19 July 1765, Boswell writes:

> At Rome I ran about among the Prostitutes till I was interrupted by that distemper [venereal disease] which scourges vice in this world. When I got to Venice I had still some small remains of disease, but strange gay ideas which I had formed of the Venetian Courtesans turned my head, and away I went to an Opera-Dancer, and took Lord Mountstuart with me. We both had her; and we both found ourselves taken in for the punishment which I had met with at Rome. Pretty doings![15]

Boswell also records paying court to a noble lady in Venice 'a little advanced in years', who refused him because she would not wish to 'take on a good cook that she could keep only for a fortnight'. He writes of other visits to Venetian courtesans, 'I fought not without glory' (*militavi non sine gloria*). In Florence, Boswell paid court to two ladies. He rejoiced of Italy, 'No longer does one have to fear the stiletto of a jealous husband'. Later, Boswell enjoyed a short affair with one of Rousseau's mistresses.

Boswell and others 'collected' sexual encounters with women from different backgrounds and places.[16] Boswell describes being 'pleased with the romantic idea of making love to a Turk'. He sought 'Saxon girls'. He went in search of the 'ugliest woman' he could find, and aimed to have a 'Swiss girl', 'an Italian countess', and a 'Florentine lady'.

Amongst Grand Tourists, Boswell's experiences were commonplace. Boswell records seeking women with his friends. They had long conversations about their favourite prostitutes and brothels. From 1570, there was a crackdown on brothels in London, and this might explain why this side of the Grand Tour became so popular. London brothels continued to exist; Boswell records visiting many of them. But prostitutes were easier to find on the continent.[17]

Philip Thicknesse's 1768 *Useful Hints to Those who Make the Tour of France* provides practical advice for debauchery:

> It is certain that men of large fortunes can in no city in the world indulge their passions in every respect more amply than in Paris; and is the lure which decoys such numbers, and in particular Englishmen, to this city of *love* and folly; and occasion such immense sums to be drained from other countries, and lavished away in debauchery of every kind.[18]

Thicknesse drily explains that Paris abounds with married women notorious for their 'devotion'. He knows a certain wife who 'spends all her mornings in prayer and confession, and all the afternoon with a young lover'.

Occasionally bear-leaders encouraged sexual engagements, as long as their charges were engaging with the 'right sort' of women. This was because some fathers saw the Grand Tour as an opportunity to educate their sons in this aspect of life. Lord Chesterfield hoped his illegitimate and unpromising son might improve through such experiences:

> The Princess of Borghese was so kind as to put him a little upon his haunches, by putting him more frequently upon her own. Nothing dresses a young fellow more than having been between such pillars, with an experienced mistress...

> *Un arrangement* which is in plain English a gallantry [sexual liaison], is, at Paris, as necessary a part of a woman of fashion's establishment, as her house, table, coach, etc. A young fellow must therefore be a very awkward one to be reduced to, or of a very singular taste, to prefer drabs [prostitutes] and danger to a commerce (in the course of the world not disgraceful) with a woman of health, education, and rank.[19]

Sex education has evolved a little since then.

> I cannot omitt setting down here an adventure that happened to Mr Dixon at the Comte de Douglass assemblée: after he had played at cards some times with Madam de Polignac: a very handsome lady: she proffered to sett him at home in her coach: which he very willingly accepted of: this young gentleman (who was a man of pleasure) finding himself alone with a fine young lady: could not forebear putting his hand where some women would not let him: after he had pleased himself thus for some time and she had bore it with a great deal of patience: she told him (in a pleasant manner) that since he had been so very free with her: she could not forbear being familiar with him: upon which she handled his arms: and finding them not fitt for present service: she beat him very heartily: he said all he could for himself: telling her that he had been upon hard duty for some time in the wars of venus: and if she would give him but one day to recruit in: he would behave himself like a man: she minded not his excuses but turned him out of the coach: and gave him this advice—
>
> Never to attack a young handsome lady as she was when his ammunition was spent.'
>
> Lord Carpenter (1717)

Sometimes the bears' debauchery went too far. One issue was that they became drunk and violent. British embassies were preoccupied by the activities of English tourists abroad.

As one onlooker put it, the tourists were 'each vying with the other who should be the wildest and most eccentric'. One traveller in Milan recorded an encounter with some Englishmen: 'last night a party of them, about a dozen, drank thirty-six bottles of burgundy, claret, and champaign...and made such a noise till six in the morning we could not sleep'. Another traveller complained about English tourists in Vienna. 'They are of the two-idea sort—The Bottle is one.'[20]

Another issue was bears sleeping with people they weren't supposed to. As Lord Chesterfield writes in his letter above, young men were supposed to pursue women of 'health, education, and rank'. To pursue other kinds of women was perceived to carry a higher risk of contracting sexually transmitted diseases. Many men died of such diseases brought home from the Tour. Many more tourists remembered their travels for years afterwards for reasons, as one historian puts it, 'that bore little relation to the restrained portraits by Batoni that decorated their libraries'. At home, these men were criticized for preferring French doctors over English ones, as the French best understood their ailments.[21]

Not only did young men pursue the wrong sort of women, they sometimes pursued other men. Italy was seen as the hotbed of homosexuality. Daniel Defoe's 1701 poem 'The True-Born Englishmen' explains that the devil 'matches proper sins for ev'ry nation'. Spain falls to pride, drunkenness 'the darling favourite of hell' rules Germany, and Russia is bound by folly. France is merely ruled by 'Ungovern'd passion', whereas:

> Lust chose the torrid zone of Italy,
> Where blood ferments in rapes and sodomy;
> Where swelling veins o'erflow with living streams.

Under the 1533 Buggery Act, sodomy was illegal in England and Wales. Convictions could result in execution. This may explain why some English noblemen, such as George Byron, chose to extend their stay on the continent, sometimes permanently.[22]

Grand Tourists also ran the risk of financial exploitation. In a 1777 letter, Thicknesse cautions a young man who is shortly to travel abroad:

> When he travels, [he should take care] to avoid the *gins and man-traps* fixed all over this country; traps, which a thorough knowledge of Latin and Greek, combined even with father's and mother's wit, will not be sufficient to preserve him from, unless he is first shown the manner in which they are set. These traps are not made to catch the legs, but to ruin the fortunes, and break the hearts of those who unfortunately step into them. Their baits are careful, designing, wicked men, and profligate, abandoned, and prostitute women. *Paris* abounds with them, as well as *Lyon,* and all the great towns between *London* and *Rome*; and they are principally set to catch the young Englishman of fortune... You suspect already, that these traps are made only of paper and ivory, and that cards and dice are the destructive engines I mean. Do you know, that there are a set of men and women, in *Paris* and *Lyons*, who live elegantly by lying in wait and by catching every *bird of passage?*—But particularly the English *gold finch.*

Beautiful women, and card sharks, scammed gentlemen out of thousands. Thicknesse concludes:

> Remember that shrewd hint of Lord Chesterfield's to his son;—'When you play with men, (says his Lordship) know with *whom* you play; when with women, for *what* you play.'—But let me add, that the only SAFE WAY, is never to play at all.[23]

Thicknesse sounds as though he is speaking from experience.

Given these problems, many writers argued against the Grand Tour. These include the philosopher Margaret Cavendish, who lived on the European continent for many years. She discusses the Grand Tour in an essay, 'An Oration concerning the Foreign Travels of Young Gentlemen'. She writes that the parents of Grand Tourists are largely deceived in their hopes and expectations. Through their travel, young men do not gain any profitable understanding or knowledge, and acquire only 'Vanity and Vice, which makes them Fools'.[24] Cavendish hints at the vices young men might acquire in the preceding essay, 'An Oration Reproving Vices'. Here, Cavendish entreats nobility to reform their excesses of 'Vanity, Luxury, Drunkeness, and Adultery'. Cavendish notes that the noblest citizens are most guilty of these crimes, because the poor have not the money to maintain these vices—'although they endeavour to the utmost of their Abilities'.

The Grand Tour remained popular for over a hundred and fifty years. As the number of travellers increased, so did the number of travel books. Mary Wollstonecraft reviewed dozens of travel books towards the end of the eighteenth century (and her remarks are caustic—of one book she writes 'we do not mean to insinuate that the work has no intrinsic merit, on the contrary, the prints are pretty'). Commenting on Francis Bacon's wish that travellers would keep a journal, Wollstonecraft writes, 'Were he now alive, he would have no reason to complain, for every inch of the continent has been described with scrupulous exactness.'[25]

In Europe, the Napoleonic Wars (1803–15) made travel difficult for a brief spell, and that marked the end of the Grand Tour as exclusive province of the rich. Travel became cheaper, and the middle classes began travelling in huge numbers.[26] They are caricatured in Coleridge's 1824 poem 'The Delinquent Travellers':

> 'What? not yet seen the coast of France!
> The folks will swear, for lack of bail,
> You've spent your last five years in jail!'
> Keep moving! Steam, or Gas, or Stage,
> Hold, cabin, steerage, hencoop's cage—
> Tour, Journey, Voyage, Lounge, Ride, Walk,
> Skim, Sketch, Excursion, Travel-talk—
> For move you must! 'Tis now the rage,
> The law and fashion of the Age.

In 1841, the English travel agency Thomas Cook arranged the first 'organized tours' around Britain. A few years later, they took tourists to Italy and the United States. (In British English, a 'Cook's Tour' is a speedy journey.) Many people were dismayed by this tourist traffic.

Here is Irish novelist Charles Lever, ranting about English tourists in Italy:

> This evil, however, has now developed itself in a form of exaggeration for which I was in no way prepared. It seems that some enterprising and unscrupulous man [Thomas Cook] has devised the project of conducting some forty or fifty persons, irrespective of age or sex, from London to Naples and back for a fixed sum. He contracts to carry them, feed them, lodge them, and amuse them...When I read the scheme first in a newspaper advertisement I caught at the hope that the speculation would break down...the characteristic independence of Englishmen would revolt against a plan that reduces the traveller to the level of his trunk, and obliterates every trace and trait of the individual. I was all wrong: the thing has 'taken'—the project is a success; and, as I write, the cities of Italy are deluged with droves of these creatures.[27]

Lever lied to one of his foreign friends about these tourists, claiming they were *convicts*. 'I told him that our Australian colonies had made such a rumpus of late about being made convict settlements, that we had adopted the cheap expedient of sending our rogues abroad to the Continent, apparently as tourists.'

It was not just travel within Europe that was increasing. Rail travel across the United States, Canada, Asia, and the Middle East began in earnest from the 1850s onwards. Faster steam ships could make the trans-Atlantic crossing in weeks, rather than months. People travelled in greater numbers through the Americas, the Middle East, and Africa. The mid twentieth century saw passenger aeroplanes, which shrank the world still further. Airplane tickets are now cheaper than ever.

Tourism has come a long way from its roots, and booms today. The United Nations World Tourism Organization estimates that internationally there were 25 million tourist arrivals in 1950, increasing to 1.2 billion international arrivals in 2016.[28] As far as I can see, as the number of tourists multiplied, their reasons for travel multiplied too.

Many people still travel to advance their educations, and for debauchery. Anthony Bourdain travelled for food; try his 2007 *No Reservations: Around the World on an Empty Stomach*. Some travel for improved social status on returning home.[29] Others travel to shop.[30] Alain de Botton's 2002 *The Art of Travel* asks why people travel at length, exploring the work of artists and writers on travel, and argues that travel allows us to bring home 'life-enhancing' thoughts.[31] These might be 'nothing more but then again nothing less' than newly appreciating architectural styles.

The twentieth-century philosopher Albert Camus travelled for fear. His travel writings are charming; here is a 1936 journal entry on the Spanish archipelago:

> *The Balearic Islands*
> The bay.
> San Fransisco—the cloister.
> Bellver.

> The wealthy district (the shadows and the old women).
> The poor district (the window).
> The cathedral (bad taste and a masterpiece).
> A cafe with a piano.

While reflecting on travel, Camus writes:

> What gives the value to travel is fear. It is the fact that, at a certain moment, when we are so far from our own country... we are seized by a vague fear, and an instinctive desire to go back to the protection of old habits. This is the most obvious benefit of travel. At that moment we are feverish but also porous, so that the slightest touch makes us quiver to the depths of our being. We come across a cascade of light, and there is eternity. This is why we should not say we travel for pleasure. There is no pleasure in travelling, and I look upon it more as an occasion for spiritual testing.[32]

For Camus, being abroad makes us afraid, and that dread opens us to the world. Continuing to travel amidst that fear and openness tests us spiritually, but the challenge is worthwhile. Sadly, Camus never travelled very far because he was motorphobic (afraid of automobiles) yet died in a car crash.

In a 2011 interview, Paul Theroux explores the 'why travel' question.[33] He is especially concerned with travel to 'maligned' countries: places subject to the 'bungling and bellicosity' of history, 'worsened by natural disasters and unprovoked cruelty'. Being a traveller in such places can be inconvenient, even fatal. Nonetheless, Theroux argues that being able to return and brag, 'I was there. I saw it all' is worth a great deal. Shocking though the travel experiences may seem at the time, they are enrichments, blessings, 'life-altering trophies of the road'. Theroux pits this kind of travel against the 'undiluted jollification' obtained by baking in the sun at Waikiki. Theroux describes recent trips to Turkmenistan and Sudan where, along with 'oppression and human rights violations', he found 'hospitality, marvels and a sense of discovery'.

Amongst this splay of tourist motivations, literature theorists have detected an intriguing trend in travel writing. From the mid twentieth century, they argue that travel writing took a 'psychological turn'. There is an increased focus on psychological issues, on the interplay between the traveller and their world.[34] Travellers make an *exterior* voyage, perhaps through Egypt or Malaysia. Side by side with this, they also make an *interior* voyage, perhaps of self-discovery or fulfilment.[35] For example, Wheeler's *Terra Incognita* describes how Antarctica helped her fight her demons. In a 2011 article, she writes:

> Antarctica was an uplifting experience—the most uplifting of my life. The only unowned continent (as well as the highest, the driest, and a battalion of other superlatives), it represents hope. No wars, no toxic spills, no dictators: this is what could have been, and what still could be, if we have hope. I found that the absence of clutter—the absence of everything—helped me reflect on what was most important. The continent was a spiritual power station.[36]

Bill Bryson's *Lost Continent* works through the death of his father. Elizabeth Gilbert's 2006 bestseller *Eat, Pray, Love: One Woman's Search for Everything across Italy, India and Indonesia* does what it says on the tin. Exterior and interior voyage go hand in hand.

A few hours later, I reached the apex of my own tourist journey: the Arctic Circle, 115 miles north of Fairbanks. This is an imaginary line circling the Earth, marking the northernmost point at which the noon sun is still visible at the December solstice. Go any further north and you'll experience 'polar night', where the sun is blotted out for at least twenty-four hours over winter.

On the Dalton Highway, the Arctic Circle is marked by a sign and a viewing deck. The sign proudly proclaims that you have reached 66°33' North. Everything south of this latitude is merely the 'northern temperate zone', whilst everything north is the Arctic proper. The first recorded visit to the Arctic was undertaken by the Greek explorer Pytheas, during the second half of the fourth century BCE. Sailing through ice seas he visits a 'frozen zone' named 'Thule', where night falls for six months of the year. Pytheas reportedly sailed north six days from northern Britain, which could just place him on the Arctic Circle. Thule *may* be Iceland.[37] In any case, on Pytheas's return to continental Europe, few people believed his reports of icy wastes.

I had the spot to myself. Trees stretched into the distance, shrinking with the road. I stepped from one side of the sign to the other, moving into the Arctic and out of it, like scores of earlier tourists. As clouds fogged the sun, I sat on a dry patch of deck and ate a supermarket salad. For the first time the raw landscape felt sad, which really meant *I* felt sad. In a few months I would be moving away from Groningen permanently, and leaving Holland grieved me. This trip was a mini departure, presaging a lasting one. Inside the salad box was a stubby fork, and I found an odd comfort in it. At least my drive to the Arctic Circle was part of a tourist tradition inherited from Coryate the Fork-Bearer.

"I'M READY"

TAKE YOUR DOG
WITH YOU BY RAIL

Return Tickets at Single Rate

DRINKING WATER FOR DOGS CAN BE OBTAINED FROM STATION REFRESHMENT
ROOMS. OR ON REQUEST TO A MEMBER OF THE STATION STAFF.

G.W.R.   LMS   L·N·E·R   S.R.

6

TRAVEL WRITING, THOUGHT EXPERIMENTS, AND MARGARET CAVENDISH'S *BLAZING WORLD*

Northerly though Alaska is, the North Pole is farther north. The Earth's geographic North Pole is the northernmost point on the planet. From the North Pole, all directions point south. The South Pole rests in Antarctica, a land mass crusted with snow. In contrast, the North Pole rides the Arctic Ocean, a magnetic point atop shifting sea ice.

Humans have been creating legends about the Poles for hundreds of years. People have variously described the Arctic as an icy region holding brutes who 'hiss like geese', and as a paradise.[1] The myth that Santa lives at the North Pole was established by an American cartoonist.

Countries keep trying to claim the Arctic, which is partly why Norwegian explorer Roald Amundsen once dropped Norwegian, Italian, and American flags over it. And why, just over a decade ago, Russia sent two submersibles 13,980 feet down to plant a rust-proof titanium flag on the seabed of the North Pole. 'As far as is known,' journalist Tim Marshall writes, 'it still "flies" down there today.'[2]

I haven't visited the geographic North Pole but I have been to North Pole, Alaska. My guidebook said the town was amusingly tacky, and that seemed a good reason to visit. North Pole did not disappoint. The town's road names include Santa Claus Lane, Snowman Lane, Mistletoe, Holiday Road, Saint Nicholas Drive, North Star Drive, Blitzen, and Donnor. Street lights and flag poles are painted as red and white candy canes. Even the McDonalds sign was striped. Santa Claus House, a gift shop, boasts the world's tallest fibreglass statue of Father Christmas. I revelled in its silliness, enjoyed every candy cane. I bought postcards of Fibreglass Santa, and the clerk sing-songed the town's slogan whilst counting my change.

'Be sure to come back, the spirit of Christmas lives year round here.'

After a while though, the jollity began to pale. After Christmas, have you ever left the decorations up a few days too long? In early January they suddenly start to feel *wrong*. With a creeping feeling, I began to see the whole town in that light: Christmas had finished four months ago, and celebrating next Christmas wasn't yet appropriate. The Yuletide decorations were out of place.

One way of understanding North Pole, Alaska, is to see it as a thought experiment. Experiments aim at discovery, by testing ideas or hypotheses. The word 'experiment' evokes scientists in white coats, working with petri dishes or particle colliders. Thought experiments are different. Thought experiments take place *inside our heads*. Philosophers have been using them for at least two thousand years. The 'trolley problem' is a famous example.[3] Imagine sitting at the controls of a railway switch. A train or trolley is hurtling down the track, completely out of control, towards a junction. At the junction, the track branches. Five people are sitting on the left-hand track, and one person is sitting on the right-hand track. If you do nothing, the train will travel on the left-hand track, and smash into five people. But, if you flip the switch, the train will change tracks and strike the lone person. What should you do?

I don't claim to know the right answer to this question.[4] The important thing is, thought experiments make us think. They can show us things about the world we didn't know before we started. Thought experiments are not just used by philosophers. They have also been used by physicists, mathematicians, and economists.[5] And, I argue, the residents of Davis, Alaska.

Although the Arctic Circle runs through it, Alaska isn't even the most northerly landmass: Denmark's Kaffeklubben Island and Canada's Qikiqtaaluk Region lie closer. Back in the 1950s, people began settling Davis, a small homestead in central Alaska. Davis was around 1,700 miles south of the geographic North Pole. Despite that distance, some of its enterprising inhabitants pondered the connection between the North Pole and Santa Claus. They wondered: What would happen if we renamed Davis 'North Pole'? They thought it through, and decided the name would attract toymakers and tourists. That would make money for the town, so they went ahead and changed the name. In the end these men of Davis were wrong about attracting toymakers, but right about drawing tourists.[6]

Many thought experiments, philosophic and otherwise, are quick to run. I've just described two thought experiments in a few sentences each. Sometimes, though, people want to run *longer* thought experiments. A simple way to do this is through fiction, especially travel fiction. One of the most interesting thought experiments can be found in the work of philosopher Margaret Cavendish, who is responding to the sense of exploration in the European air, ideas about the North Pole, and Bacon's new views on science. Before we can enter Cavendish's Blazing World, we need to understand the world of travel writing and philosophical thought experiments more generally.

'Fiction' is invented. Jane Austen's *Pride and Prejudice*. J. R. R. Tolkien's *Lord of the Rings*. J. K. Rowling's *Harry Potter and the Philosopher's Stone*. These fictional novels describe imaginary places or people. We usually think that travel books are 'non-fiction', like newspaper articles or scientific reports. Aren't they describing real places and real people? In fact, this isn't always the case. Travel books often blur the line between fiction and non-fiction.

Consider travel books like Bill Bryson's *Lost Continent* or John Gimlette's *Wild Coast*. These books are presented as works of non-fiction, yet they make use of many fictional devices. They use metaphor and hyperbole. Flying over the Essequibo River, Gimlette looks down over landscape shaped 'like the spines of books'. They have plots that flash backwards or forwards, often with a twist at the end. They exaggerate, parody, satirize. Bryson describes one remote hamlet, 'Dog Water' or 'Dunceville', as the kind of place where if a dog gets run over by a truck 'everybody gets out to have a look at it'.

In early travel books, lots of content was fabricated. Remember Mandeville's *Travels*, and the islanders who have heads like dogs? This sort of thing led Francis Bacon and others to ask that travellers write truthfully. We can arrange travel writing on a spectrum, from less fictional to more fictional—see Figure 6.1.

At the non-fictional end are 'scientific' travel books. These include James Cook and Charles Darwin's books (although even these use some fictional devices). At the fictional end are books that appear to be real-world reports, yet are mostly unreal. These include Thomas More's 1516 *Utopia*, Joseph Hall's 1605 *Another World and Yet the Same*, Aphra

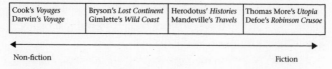

| Cook's *Voyages* | Bryson's *Lost Continent* | Herodotus' *Histories* | Thomas More's *Utopia* |
| Darwin's *Voyage* | Gimlette's *Wild Coast* | Mandeville's *Travels* | Defoe's *Robinson Crusoe* |

Non-fiction ← — — — — — — — — — — — — — — → Fiction

Figure 6.1 *A spectrum of travel writing*

Behn's 1688 *Oroonoko: Or, The Royal Slave,* and Daniel Defoe's 1719 *Robinson Crusoe.*

Fictional travel books like *Robinson Crusoe* borrow devices from non-fiction ones. They are written in a plain style, and set in real-world places like the Caribbean.[7] (After publication, many readers believed the events of *Robinson Crusoe* happened.) A novel imitating a real travel report gains credibility and depth. This makes it attractive to philosophers. If you want to build a complex thought experiment, how better than to write a fictional travel book? The idea of writing philosophical thought experiments as travel books is an old one. We're going to explore three such books, starting with Thomas More's *Utopia*.

The statesman and philosopher Thomas More is perhaps best known for being beheaded. Before this unfortunate occurrence, More published a travel book: his 1516 *On the Best Kind of a Republic and About the New Island of Utopia* (*De optimo rei publicae deque nova insula Utopia*).

Utopia is a novel masquerading as a non-fiction travel book. It describes the sea voyages of a young man, Raphael Hythlodaeus, off the coast of South America. Having sailed past Brazil, Hythlodaeus discovered the island of Utopia—shown in Figure 6.2. He spends five years there, and reports on all aspects of life. Hythlodaeus tells us that Utopia is in the middle two hundred miles broad, and holds almost the same breadth over a great part of it, but grows narrower towards both ends. It contains fifty-four cities, all large and

Figure 6.2 *A map of Utopia*

well built, the manners, customs, and laws of which are the same. The inhabitants use punishment to frighten men off committing crimes, and invite them to the love of virtue by public honours. To the memories of worthy men who have served their country well, they erect statues in the marketplace.[8]

We discover that Utopians engage in many controversial practices. They allow female priests and married priests. They allow people to divorce. They allow euthanasia, the mercy killing of people suffering from incurable conditions. *Utopia* is a thought experiment: More is exploring a society divergent from his own.

The word 'utopia' is Greek, and it is a joke on More's part: it means 'no-place'. Like travel books, utopian stories abounded during the European Age of Discovery. Scholars have argued this is no coincidence. Travel books and utopias both portray difference. They both involve physical journeys to reach new lands. They also both involve more metaphorical journeys: encounters with new peoples and new ideas. Further, travel books and utopias are both 'reflexive'. They purport to show foreign places but really encourage readers to reflect on their home places. Travel books and utopias feed off each other. Utopias are modelled on travel books, and travellers searched for utopias.

After More's *Utopia*, the word 'utopia' came to mean any non-existent and ideal society. These include Cyrano de Bergerac's 1657 *Histoire comique contenant les États et Empires de la lune*, and H. G. Wells's 1905 *A Modern Utopia*. The twentieth century saw a wave of *dys*topias, non-existent and non-ideal societies. Aldous Huxley's 1931 *Brave New World*. George Orwell's 1949 *Nineteen Eighty-Four*. Margaret Atwood's 1985 *The Handmaid's Tale*. The trend continues today, with Suzanne Collins's 2008 *Hunger Games* and Naomi Alderman's 2016 *The Power*. I don't know what this says about us.

More's *Utopia* inspired many more utopian tales, including one by our old friend Francis Bacon. Apparently, Bacon intended his fictional travel book *New Atlantis*[9] to be a 'companion' for his latest non-fiction work on natural history, *Sylva Sylvarum*. Although Bacon does not explain why he wrote *New Atlantis*, it acts as a thought experiment. Bacon seems to be showing us the good things that will happen if we adopt his scientific methods: we will produce a utopia.

According to Plato, Atlantis is a lost realm. It is somewhere beyond the Pillars of Hercules, in the realm of the Unknown. In Bacon's tale, a group of travellers discover a new Atlantis. The travellers are sailing in the South Seas, off the coast of Peru, when a tempest forces them to land on the island of Bensalem.

Bensalem is the new Atlantis. The islanders are well mannered, chaste, and civilized. They are also very happy, their lives improved through knowledge and technology. At the heart of their island is a scientific research centre called 'Salomon's House'. Their host tells them that this House is dedicated to the study of the works and creatures of God, and they possess Salomon's natural history 'of all plants, from the cedar of Libanus to the moss that groweth out of the wall, and of all things that have life and motion'. Bacon draws parallels between Bensalem's House of Salomon and Jerusalem's Temple of Solomon. The subtext is that our world, and the Temple of Solomon, will be renewed through science. Indeed, when Robert Hooke and others created the Royal Society, some saw that as the realization of Bacon's House of Salomon.[10]

With this background in place, we're ready to dig into the most creative travel thought experiment I know of: Margaret Cavendish's 1666 *Description of a New World, Called The Blazing-World*.[11] This novel is both philosophically clever and engagingly bizarre.

Before the twentieth century it was rare for women to practise philosophy. Women seldom received much education in philosophy or science, and writing was discouraged. Margaret Cavendish née Lucas (1623–73) was a rare early woman philosopher.

Margaret was born in Essex, the youngest child of eight. Although she did not receive a formal education in mathematics or philosophy, she was an avid reader with access to libraries. She discussed philosophy with her brother John Lucas (who would later become a founding member of the Royal Society). Even in her early years, Margaret relished 'scribbling' down her own thoughts. She also enjoyed making her own clothes.

Her family life was upset in 1641, when anti-royalists attacked the family home. In 1642, Margaret and her mother retreated to Oxford, where King Charles I held his court. In 1643, Margaret became maid of honour to Charles's wife, Queen Henrietta Maria. In 1644, during the English Civil War, the Queen sought refuge in France, and Margaret followed her. Margaret soon met another royalist in exile, William Cavendish the Marquis of Newcastle. They married in 1645 and remained in exile together, residing in Paris, Rotterdam, and Antwerp. When Charles II was restored to the English throne in 1660, they could return. After a brief stint in London, they retired to their estate at Welbeck.

William supported his wife's work and brought her into contact with many philosophers, including Descartes, Thomas Hobbes, Marin Mersenne, Pierre Gassendi, and Kenelm Digby. (Incidentally, Digby was an English privateer as well as a philosopher, and spent several years attacking Dutch and Spanish ships on the high seas.) With her husband's help, Cavendish published theatre plays and philosophy books. In 1667, she accepted a rare invitation to take part in a meeting of the scientific Royal Society. She was the first woman to do so, and it became an event of high spectacle. In advance of her visit, scientists spent over a week preparing experiments for her to view. They included 'the mixing of cold liquors, which upon their infusion grew hot'. A 'terrella', a miniature magnetized globe, that drove 'away the steel-dust at its poles'. Also 'the dissolving of meat in the oil of vitriol'.

The diarist Samuel Pepys recorded several sightings of Cavendish. In an entry dated 11 April 1667, Pepys writes of one of her London visits:

> The whole story of this Lady is a romance, and all she doth is romantic. Her footmen in velvet coats, and herself in an

antique dress, as they say; and was the other day at her own
play, *The Humorous Lovers*; the most ridiculous thing that
ever was wrote, but yet she and her Lord mightily pleased
with it, and she at the end made her respect to the players
from her box and did them thanks. There is as much
expectation of her coming to Court, that so [many] people
may come to see her, as if it were the Queen of Sweden.[12]

This reference to Cavendish's fashion sense was not
uncommon. Cavendish's autobiography explains that as a
child she preferred 'variety of fine clothes' to toys. She
'did dislike any should follow my fashions, for I always
took delight in a singularity'. In Pepys's entry on Cavendish's
famous visit to the Royal Society, he focuses again on her
clothes. Pepys writes, 'her dress so antic and her deportment
so unordinary, that I do not like her at all, nor did I hear
her say anything that was worth hearing'. In her day,
Cavendish was variously regarded as a genius, and as quite
mad. In the 1660s she acquired a nickname, 'Mad Madge'.
After her death she was buried at Westminster Abbey.[13]

Alongside plays and philosophy, Cavendish wrote a science
fiction novel—perhaps the first ever authored by a woman.
Blazing World tells the story of a young lady collecting shells
on a seashore, when she is kidnapped by a lovestruck mer-
chant and carried off to sea. The heavens frown on the mer-
chant's theft, and raise a tempest. The storm forces the boat
into the icy seas around the North Pole.

The ship's crew freezes to death but, protected by the
gods, the Lady remains alive. When the boat reaches the
North Pole, something even stranger happens:

They were not only driven to the very end or point of the
Pole of that World, but even to another Pole of another
World, which joined close to it; so that the cold having a
double strength at the conjunction of those two Poles, was

> insupportable: At last, the Boat still passing on, was forced
> into another World.

This icy new world is illuminated by alien suns. It is literally a blazing world.

Cavendish's *Blazing World* is part of the legend-making tradition about the North Pole. Myth-making thrived during her period, and many travel books discussed the North Pole. In part, this was because explorers were trying to find the 'Northwest Passage'. This fabled route would allow traders to sail from Europe to Asia via the Arctic Ocean. (The exploration went on a long time: Roald Amundsen traversed the Northwest Passage for the first time in 1903–6.) Richard Hakluyt's 1589–1600 *Principal Navigations* includes several discussions of the Passage. This one is by geographer Richard Willes:

> If any such passage be, it lies subject unto ice and snow for
> the most part of the year, where it stands in the edge of the
> frostie zone. Before the Sunne hath warmed the air, and dis-
> solved the ice, each one [explorer] well knows that there can
> be no sailing…how shall it be possible for so weak a vessel
> as a ship is, to hold out amid whole Islands, as it were of ice
> continually beating on each side, and at the mouth of that
> gulf, issuing down furiously from the north, and safely to
> pass, when whole mountaines of ice and snow shall be tum-
> bled down upon her?[14]

Figure 6.3[15] shows how far the Passage had been explored in 1631.

Literature professor Line Cottegnies suggests that, in *Blazing World*, the lady's ship may sail through the Northwest Passage to reach the North Pole. Through travel books, Cavendish could have been familiar with stories of ship crews freezing. Cavendish may also have been offering a 'fanciful answer' to a map puzzle. How should we represent the Poles on maps? In reality, our

Figure 6.3 *The Northwest Passage in 1631*

planet is three-dimensional, so the Poles merely mark points on a globe. Yet, on two-dimensional maps, the Poles often appear at the north and south borders. As such, they seem to be marking the known limit of our world. Some seventeenth-century maps represented the Poles as stars, radiating longitudinal lines of light. This may be another reason why Cavendish names her world 'blazing'.[16]

Once through the North Pole, the temperature onboard the ship rises. The sailors' corpses begin to putrefy. The Lady tries to push the bodies overboard but finds them too heavy. She is saved from their 'nauseous smell' by the arrival of some creatures walking over the ice. These creatures stand upright like men yet resemble bears. The Bear-men help the Lady off the ship and decide to make her a 'Present' to their world's Emperor. On meeting the Lady, the Emperor rejoices and marries her. He gives her 'an absolute power to rule and govern all that World as she pleased'.

Now an Empress, the Lady sets about meeting her subjects, and ruling her state. From this point on, the philosophical aspects of *Blazing World* emerge. This travel book is a utopia, like those of More and Bacon. It is *also* a thought experiment, designed to attack Baconian science.

You may have gleaned the impression from this book that Bacon's philosophy of science innovations passed unopposed. However, they did not. Cavendish is one philosopher who attacked Bacon's new ideas about science, and her sallies are cutting.

Cavendish did not attack all aspects of travel or science. Although she does not value the Grand Tour, she does value travel more generally. Amongst Cavendish's fiction is a collection of 'Speeches by Dying Persons'. This collection includes a speech from a foreign traveller given (you guessed it) whilst dying. The traveller proclaims, 'Travellers have most reason to Adore and Worship God Best, for they see Most of his Wonderfull works.'[17] Like Bacon, Cavendish seems to believe that travel can help us understand God's creation.

In a 1663 essay on animal and vegetable farming, Cavendish is positive towards science. She praises the way some men have learned about soils, the weather, and growing seasons. The essay argues for the importance of men who:

> Have not only Experience by Practice, and Judgment by Observations, but have both Learning and Conceptions of Natural Philosophy, as to Learn and Search into the Causes and Effects of Natures Works, and to Know and Observe the Influences of the Heavens on Earth, and on the Diverse and Sundry Creatures In and On the Earth; also the Sympathies and Antipathies of the several Creatures to Each other, as also the Natures and Properties of every Kind and Sort of Creature.

So far, Cavendish's remarks are in lockstep with Bacon's sentiments. But she continues:

> So shall we know how to Increase our Breed of Animals, and our Stores of Vegetables, and to find out the Minerals for our Use.[18]

Cavendish is saying, science is important because it is *useful* to us. Over the next few years, she develops this position into a philosophy of science.

Cavendish's 1666 *Observations upon Experimental Philosophy* is a four-hundred-page attack on particular sciences. We'll focus on her objections to the sciences around microscopes. 'Microscopy' uses microscopes to investigate things invisible to the human eye, whilst 'micrography' is sketching such things. Back then, microscopy and micrography were relatively new. They were just beginning to attain popularity, thanks to Robert Hooke's 1665 *Micrographia: or Some physiological descriptions of minute bodies made by magnifying glasses*. Hooke's book was acclaimed by the scientific Royal Society, becoming one of its signature texts.[19] *Micrographia's* preface explains that this work continues the experimentalist project. Through microscopes, we can enlarge 'the dominion' of narrow and infirm human senses. Humans will discover the composition, structure, and inner motions of bodies. Hooke believed this will lead to 'admirable advantages' in mechanical knowledge.

Many people found Hooke's work wondrous. Under the microscope, the point of a sharp needle appears broad and blunt, its sleek surface hiding 'a multitude of holes and scratches and ruggednesses'. Punctuation marks made by different pens, like full stops or commas, appear the same to the naked eye. Yet, under the microscope, each of these '*smutty daubings*' is unique. Figure 6.4 provides Hooke's

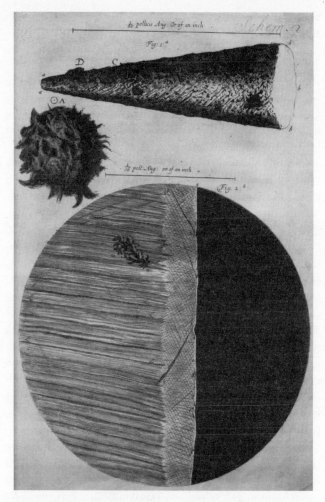

Figure 6.4 *Hooke's Micrographia*

sketch of a full stop. A razor edge looks smooth, until the microscope reveals it to be uneven and scratched.

For all this, Cavendish did not find Hooke's work wondrous. She attacks it on several grounds. First, she objects that this new science is *not* able to discover the interior motions of things. It cannot even portray their *exterior* shapes and motions:

> As for example; art makes cylinders, concave and convex glasses, and the like, which represent the figure of an object in no part exactly and truly, but very deformed and misshaped: also a glass that is flawed, cracked, or broke, or cut into the figure of lozenges, triangles, squares, or the like, will present numerous pictures of one object. Besides, there are so many alterations made by several lights, their shadows, refractions...the truth of an object will hardly be known; for the perception of sight, and so of the rest of the senses, goes no further than the exterior parts of the object presented; and though the perception may be true, when the object is truly presented, yet when the presentation is false, the information must be false also...For example; a louse by the help of a magnifying glass appears like a lobster, where the microscope enlarging and magnifying each part of it, makes them bigger and rounder than naturally they are.[20]

The illustrations in Hooke's *Micrographia* include a louse.

Why does Cavendish believe the microscope can't accurately represent things? There are several reasons. One is that microscopes are sometimes flawed. If a mirror is dented or cracked, it produces deformed reflections. Similarly, if microscope glasses are deformed or cracked, they produce a deformed image. Seventeenth-century microscopes were frequently flawed, as Cavendish well knew. She read extensively about microscopes and, with her husband's help, acquired lots of practical experience. During their exile in Paris, the pair acquired a collection of microscopes. William nicknamed his wife's microscope 'my Lady's multiplying glass'.

Another reason Cavendish believes microscopes are inaccurate is that when we look at something through them, we are not looking directly at it. Instead, we are looking at the thing *projected onto glass*. We are looking at a copy of a thing, not the thing itself. When sketching these things, we are making 'copies from copies'. This leads to mistakes. Cavendish points us towards art. Artists acknowledge that objects can possess different shapes, according to the reflections and positions of the lights around them. Consequently, it is hard to know what shape an object really has. One of the artists Cavendish has in mind is likely Hooke himself. *Micrographia*'s preface writes that, unlike bodies visible to the naked eye, it is difficult to discover the 'true shape' of microscopic bodies. The same object can seem 'quite differing, in one position to the light, from what it really is'. Locke's *Essay Concerning Human Understanding*, published over twenty years later, would raise similar concerns. For example, in one passage Locke remarks, 'Blood to the naked Eye appears all red; but by a good Microscope, wherein its lesser parts appear, shews only some few Globules of Red, swimming in a pellucid Liquor.'[21] Given the dates, it is possible that Locke read Cavendish.

In effect, Cavendish is preaching caution. *Micrographia*'s drawings imply that 'seeing' objects through microscopes is straightforward. It is just the same as using our eyes. Against this, Cavendish is arguing microscopes may *never* accurately represent things.

For Cavendish, microscopes and other new Baconian sciences are 'superficial wonders'. *This* is what she aims to show in *Blazing World*. Remember how Bacon pairs *New Atlantis* with his non-fiction *Sylva Sylvarum*? In the same way, Cavendish pairs *Blazing World* with her *Observations upon*

Experimental Philosophy. She describes the books as 'joined together', like two worlds at two Poles. There are other parallels between *New Atlantis* and *Blazing World*. One scholar has argued Cavendish modelled her utopia on Bacon's deliberately, to better highlight the disagreements between them.[22]

Armed with this background, we are ready to return to *Blazing World*. The Lady discovers many kinds of men there. As Empress, she divides them into societies. The Bear-men become her experimental philosophers, the Bird-men her astronomers. The Fly-men, Worm-men, and Fish-men become her natural philosophers, the Ape-men her chemists, the Satyrs her physicians, the Fox-men her politicians. The Spider- and Lice-men become her Mathematicians. An assortment of Bird-men, including jackdaws, magpies, and parrots, become her orators and logicians. Once divided into societies, the Lady asked them questions, such as:

- What is the nature of thunder and lightning?
- What are the motes of the sun?
- What stars are there?
- What is the air?
- How is snow made?
- Why is the sea salty?

These questions are reminiscent of Bacon's list of topics requiring scientific study. Although the Empress's subjects attempt to answer them, they rarely do so to her satisfaction.

For example, the Bird-men astronomers cannot agree on the nature of thunder and lightning. The Empress turns away from their 'tedious disputes', to the Bear-men experimentalists. She commands the Bear-men to observe the celestial bodies through their telescopes. Unfortunately, these telescopes cause 'more differences and divisions'. Some of the Bear-men perceived the sun to move, whilst others didn't. Further Bear-men fell into disputes over the size of stars. As they argued, the Empress grew angry. Why didn't their telescopes provide knowledge? The Empress continues:

> Now I do plainly perceive, that your Glasses are false Informers, and instead of discovering the Truth, delude your Senses; Wherefore I Command you to break them, and let the Bird-men trust onely to their natural eyes, and examine Cœlestial Objects by the motions of their own Sense and Reason.

The Bear-men were anguished by this. They begged that their telescopes remain unbroken, pleading they took 'more delight in Artificial delusions, than in Natural truths'. The Empress allowed them to keep their telescopes. In return, the Bear-men showed her their microscopes.

They show the Empress many objects found in Hooke's *Micrographia*, including the eye of a fly, charcoal, and a nettle leaf. Alas, the display does not go as planned, and the Empress swoons at an enlarged louse. Afterwards she asks: Could microscopes help people avoid being bitten by lice or fleas? The Bear-men say they cannot help, and the Empress is displeased. Their studies serve no useful purpose. The Empress instructs another group of creatures, 'I will not have you to take more pains, and waste your time in such fruitless attempts, but be wiser hereafter, and busie your selves with such Experiments as may be beneficial to the publick'.

Blazing World is a thought experiment. It shows what would happen if experimental science ran amok: disputes, arguments, and time wasting. For Cavendish, we should pursue science that helps human beings. Cavendish's *Observations* concludes her remarks on microscopes:

> But could experimental philosophers find out more benefi-
> cial arts than our forefathers have done, either for the bet-
> ter increase of vegetables and brute animals to nourish our

bodies, or better and commodious contrivances in the art of architecture to build us houses, or for the advancing of trade and traffic to provide necessaries for us to live...it would not only be worth their labour, but of as much praise as could be given to them: But, as boys that play with watery bubbles or fling dust into each other's eyes, or make a hobbyhorse of snow, are worthy of reproof rather than praise, for wasting their time with useless sports; so those that addict themselves to unprofitable arts, spend more time than they reap benefit thereby.[23]

In the twenty-first century, there are many more sciences. Lots of these are not obviously useful for humans. Does it improve our lives to know how many galaxies there are, or how electrons work? One counter argument is that these sciences may yield useful technologies or ideas in the future.

Hooke and Cavendish didn't know that microscopy could be useful. Today, we know microscopy has oodles of uses. Traditional optical microscopes analyse tissue cells and bacteria. This helps us to diagnose medical conditions more quickly, and develop new drugs. Electron microscopes help us to create silicon microchips. These power computers, smartphones, and the internet. Scanning acoustic microscopes detect cracks in metals, making aircraft panels safer. If Cavendish could have looked into the future, I think the Empress would have praised the Bear-men's microscopes.

Blazing World provides a thought experiment about the philosophy of science. Before leaving it, I want to explore one last question. How unreal is the Blazing World?

My tale of candy canes in North Pole, Alaska, is non-fiction and real. Cavendish's tale of the kidnapped young lady sailing to the magnetic North Pole is fiction and unreal. Yet, for Cavendish, her Blazing World is both fictional *and* real. Explaining how requires a bit of background.

Cavendish believes everything around us is 'material'. Everything is made of matter, the same stuff that makes up human bodies and trees and moons. Although this view is commonplace today, in her time it was controversial, partly because it eliminated the immaterial human soul. Unlike other philosophers, Cavendish doesn't believe that matter is inert. Instead, all matter is alive, and 'self-moving'. Humans are nothing special, merely parts of a grand material system. An oak is composed of living, moving matter, and so is a human mind. A mind and its ideas is just a system of moving matter.

For Cavendish, there is a deep similarity between the world and our minds. Both are patterns of moving matter. She reflects on the similarities in this poem, 'Similizing the Head of Man to the World':

> As twinckling *Stars* shew in dark *Clouds,* that's cleare,
> So *Fancies* quick do in the *Braine* appeare...
> Just as the *Earth,* the *Heads* round *Ball,*
> Is crown'd with *Orbes Coelestiall.*
> So *Head,* and *World* as one agree;
> *Nature* did make the *Head* a *World* to bee.

In our imaginations, we can create worlds inside our heads. Thomas More created Utopia, and J. K. Rowling created Hogwarts. Given Cavendish's view that our minds and ideas are material, the only difference between the real world and the worlds we imagine is in their size. The real world is enormous, whereas fictional worlds inside our heads are small. Nonetheless, our imaginary worlds are just miniature versions of the real world.

Blazing World opens with a poem from Cavendish's husband:

> *Columbus then for Navigation fam'd,*
> *Found a new World, America 'tis nam'd;*

Now this one World was found, it was not made...
But your creating Fancy, thought it fit
To make your World of Nothing, but pure Wit.

(William Newcastle, *To the Duchess of Newcastle,
on her Blazing World*)

Here, William argues that his wife's achievements outshine
those of Europe's best-known explorers. Columbus only
'discovered' a new world, whereas Cavendish has *created* one.

This provides another level on which *Blazing World* is
working. On its surface, it is a travel book about a young
lady who travels through the North Pole. Below that, it is a
thought experiment showing how foolish Baconian science
can be. Go deeper still, and it is *literally* a travel book:
Cavendish is describing a world just as real as our own. The
Empress's palace is as real as Santa Claus House, Alaska.

7

MOUNTAIN TRAVEL AND HENRY MORE'S PHILOSOPHY OF SPACE

Exultation is the going
Of an inland soul to sea,
Past the houses, past the headlands,
Into deep eternity.

Emily Dickinson, 'Exultation is the going' (*c*,1860)

Alaska is riddled with mountains. If someone made a paper cutout of the landmass and crumpled it, they couldn't do any better. Like most tourists, Anchorage was the first place I saw in Alaska, and it's filled with mountains. Flying in, your plane windows crowd with white, jagged riffs, cartoonish triangles stacked against each other.

Downtown Anchorage feels surrounded, a puff of humanity cradled by rock. From Cook Monument I looked across to Mount Susitna, known in English as the 'Sleeping Lady' (in Dena'ina it's *Dghelishla*, Little Mountain). James Cook never actually set foot here, he merely surveyed the coastline in his fruitless search for the Northwest Passage. Yet his statue stands tall, looking determined with a roll of maps under one arm, staring at waters running out into the open sea. ('Alaska' comes from the Aleut *Aldxsxaq*—'The object toward which the action of the sea is directed'.)[1]

From Anchorage, I climbed Flattop Mountain. It was a murky afternoon, sky blocked out in Payne's grey. Eastward lay the Chugach Mountains. At 250 miles long and 60 miles wide, this range is roughly the size of Switzerland. It receives more snowfall than anywhere else in the world. Its tallest mount, at 13,094 feet, is named after Marcus Baker, a geologist who mapped parts of Alaska. Other memorable names include Bashful Peak, Icing Peak, Polar Bear Peak, Mount Valhalla, and North Suicide Peak. These mountain teeth glowed white, whilst smudges that might have been Mount Foraker or Denali loomed on the skyline. I shivered and retreated downwards. I wouldn't see Denali properly until I boarded the *Aurora Winter* the next day.

Denali is North America's tallest mountain, topping 20,310 feet. It spires over the Alaska Range and Denali National Park, visible from over a hundred miles away. James Michener called it 'the glory of Alaska'. The 'Great One' is so big it creates its own weather. Storms from the Gulf of Alaska and the Bering Sea barrel into Denali, spawning blizzards and snow. When I first laid eyes on it, I didn't just feel small. I felt *brief*. The average human lives for seventy years. Denali is several hundred *million* years old.

Although mountains grow at a glacial rate (pun intended) Western ideas about mountains have evolved rapidly. Medieval and seventeenth-century thinkers characterized mountains as dangerous, dark, and ugly. In the eighteenth century, mountains became beautiful, majestic, and cathedral-like. What changed? The answer lies partly in a new theory of space, advanced in the 1670s by Henry More.

The mountain–space connection was first made by American literary scholar Marjorie Hope Nicolson, in her 1959 *Mountain Gloom, Mountain Glory*. This thoughtful book explores shifts in Western attitudes towards mountains. Nicolson presents various texts showing how early thinkers characterized mountains negatively.[2] For example, here is the entry in Joshua Poole's 1657 handbook for poets:

Mountain.

Moss-thrum'd, rocky, shady, cloud-headed, insolent, steep, ambitious, towring, aspiring, mossie, hoary, aged, steepy, surly, burly, lofty, tall, craggy, barren, stately, climbing, sky-killing, sky-threatening, cloud-inwrapped, high-browed, shaggy, supercilious, air-invading, hanging, brambly, desert, uncouth, solitary...thorny, inhospitable, shady, cold, freezing, unfruitful, lovely, crump-shouldered, ragged, unfrequented, forsaken, melancholy.[3]

I especially like 'crump-shouldered', although disappointingly 'crump' means 'hunched' rather than 'crumpet-like'.

There are a few positive associations here: aspiring, stately, lovely. But the overwhelming majority are negative: insolent, surly, barren, sky-killing. As Nicolson explains, Poole's negative characterization of mountains was commonplace. John Donne's 1611 poem 'Anatomy of the world' describes mountains as 'warts, and pock-holes on the face of th' earth'.

I have found similar sentiments in the letters of Irish philosopher George Berkeley. In his twenties and early thirties he spent several years travelling around the European continent, sometimes as a bear-leader. He twice crossed Mount Cenis, a French–Italian mountain pass, in winter. Of the 1714 crossing, Berkeley describes 'a perpetual chain of rocks and mountains', rocks and precipices high and craggy enough 'to cause the heart of the most valiant man to melt'. (He adds that he only fell off his horse four times, breaking sword, watch, and snuffbox.) Berkeley claims the 1716 crossing was even worse: the pass blowing, bitter, its precipices 'horrid'. One of his mountain anecdotes is particularly memorable:

A huge dark coloured alpine wolf ran across an open plain when our chaise was passing, when he came near as he

> turned about and made a stand with a very fierce and marking look, I instantly drew my sword and Mr. Ashe fired his pistol. I did the same too, upon which the beast very calmly retired and looking back ever and anon.[4]

Philosopher intimidates wolf with sword.

Having argued that early moderns conceived mountains as horrid, dangerous places, Nicolson goes on to argue that the nineteenth century saw an attitude shift. For example, here is Byron's 1812 description of mountains in *Childe Harold's Pilgrimage*:

> Above me are the Alps,
> The palaces of Nature, whose vast walls
> Have pinnacled in clouds their snowy scalps,
> And thron'd Eternity in icy halls
> Of cold sublimity, where forms and falls
> The avalanche—the thunderbolt of snow!
> *All that expands the spirit, yet appals*
> Gather around these summits.

In a poem about Rome's St Peter's Basilica, Byron compares the dome to a mountain:

> But lo, the dome, the vast and wondrous dome...
> Thou moves—but increasing with the advance,
> Like climbing some great Alp, which still doth rise,
> Deceived by its gigantic elegance;
> Vastness which grows, but grows to harmonise—
> All musical in its immensities.

Bryon was not alone. In the 1800s, many thinkers were describing mountains positively. The painter John Ruskin wrote of the Alps, 'Great cathedrals of the earth, with their gates of rock, pavements of cloud, choirs of stream and stone, altars of snow, and vaults of purple traversed by the continual stars'.

In 1858, Elena Ghika wrote of the Alps:

> The image of the infinite presented itself to my mind in all its formidable grandeur. My oppressed heart felt it, as I gazed on the Swiss plains, lost in the mist, and the neighbouring mountains which were covered with golden vapours. I conceived such an idea of God that it appeared to me I had never before that day given him sufficient place in my heart.[5]

We can even find such positive descriptions of Alaskan mountains. In his 1915 *Travels through Alaska*, the Scottish-American naturalist John Muir, aka 'John of the Mountains', describes a sunrise in the Fairweather Mountains:

> We were startled by the sudden appearance of a red light burning with a strange earthly splendour on the topmost peak...it spread and spread until the whole range down to the level of the glaciers was filled with the celestial fire. In colour it was at first a vivid crimson, with a thick, furred appearance, as fine as the alpenglow, yet indescribably rich and deep...

> The white, rayless light of morning, seen when I was alone amid the peeks of the California Sierra, had always seemed to me the most telling of all the terrestrial manifestations of God. But here the mountains themselves were made divine, and declared His glory in terms still more impressive.[6]

One of Alaska's glaciers is actually named after Muir.

What prompted this shift, from mountain gloom to mountain glory? Mountains are rumpled jags of rock, inhospitable and inhuman. A brute like Denali is not obviously cathedral-like. Nicolson argues the change is rooted in the philosophy of space. More specifically, in a theory first advanced by Henry More.

You've probably never heard of More. Yet, in the seventeenth century, he was one of Britain's leading philosophers. Through my work on the history of philosophy, I have spent a lot of time with More. He lived almost his entire life at Christ's College, Cambridge, and witnessed some of the most difficult events England has ever seen. The intermittent Civil War. Outbreaks of the Black Death. Comets that were believed to herald the apocalypse. Despite all this, More managed to write lots of books, and he thought deeply about space.

Consider space. I don't mean 'outer space', where the stars and galaxies are. I mean space as in 'spacetime', or the space inside an empty box. More investigated the metaphysics of space. He wanted to know: What *is* space?

At the time More was writing, two theories of space were popular.[7] One is 'void theory'. This comes from the classical Greek atomists. For example, Democritus claimed, 'in truth there are only atoms and the void'. In the early seventeenth century, the French philosopher Gassendi resurrected Greek atomism. Gassendi conceived space as a kind of unreal being, a void or nothingness. Atoms and bodies move about inside this void.

The other theory is 'Aristotelian'. This comes from Aristotle, who rejected the atomist conception of space. On the atomist view, material bodies occupy a 'magnitude', an area of void space. For example, a cube of wood would take up an area measuring several cubic inches. Yet Aristotle argues the cube already has a magnitude *of its own*. If the cube is four inches long on each side, then it has a magnitude of four inches square. Consequently, Aristotle argues we do not need a void space to put the cube in. The cube carries its own space with it. Descartes revived Aristotle's view. Descartes discusses the 'extension' of material bodies, the cube's breadth, width, and depth. He argues the cube's extension is identical with the extension of the space it takes up.[8] Consider the cube in Figure 7.1. Is the cube

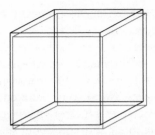

Figure 7.1 *How does this cube relate to the space it takes up?*

located in space? Or, through its breadth, width, and depth, is the cube already spatial? For Descartes, a material body is always spatial, so wherever there is body, there is already space. This also means that, for Descartes, there is no space empty of matter. Wherever there is space, there is matter.

More's views on space developed over the course of his career. The position he finally reached is a solution to two problems. The first problem is: What is the relationship between space and matter? More read Descartes carefully. Although More was impressed by Descartes' work, he could not accept Descartes' account of space. For More, it was possible to have empty spaces, spaces that are empty of matter. Unlike Descartes, More believed that if we removed all material bodies from the world, there would still be space left behind.

The second problem is: What is God's relationship with the world? For Descartes, the universe is like a giant machine. Initially, More found this idea very attractive. It allowed him to jettison older, more mysterious theories about what the world is. In the end, though, More concluded that Descartes' philosophy led to atheism. Descartes' mechanistic picture didn't seem to need God in it. God could have created the world machine and then ambled off. Even if God hung around, there was no *need* for him to exist in the created world. More rejected such views, and describes the theory that God is nowhere as 'a vast great mound of darkness'.

Gradually, More's thoughts on these problems converged. More had long believed that space is infinite, and was in awe of it. Here is an excerpt from one of his earliest poems:

> Wherefore with leave th'infinite I'll sing
> Of Time, of Space: or without leave; I'm brent
> With eagre rage, my heart for joy doth spring,
> And all my spirits move with pleasant trembeling.[9]

More is 'singing' with joy about infinite time and space. He became convinced that space would exist, even if there were no material bodies. More's greatest work, his 1671 *Manual of Metaphysics (Enchiridion Metaphysicum),* is deeply concerned with space (Figure 7.2).

More argues 'a certain immobile extension' is everywhere. This space is 'distinct from mobile matter'. For More, space is an infinite, eternal 'container'. As in Figure 7.2, space contains material bodies.[10] Space would exist even if there were nothing inside it.

For More, this extension is not nothing. He reasons this extension must *belong* to something, in the same way a cube's extension belongs to the cube. More argues this infinite extension belongs to God. He points out that space shares at least twenty of God's titles. Space and God are both unmoving, independent, complete, and eternal. More concludes that a thing so 'decorated' with divine names cannot be unreal. It is not 'mere space'. It is a 'certain substance'—the immaterial substance of God.[11] More is identifying space with God's omnipresence, the everywhere-ness of God. This was a radical solution but it solved both More's philosophical problems. It explained why time and space

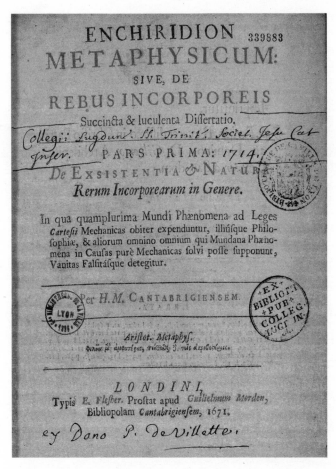

Figure 7.2 *The title page of More's Enchiridion Metaphysicum*

could exist without material bodies, and it stationed God in the world.

More's new theory, that space is God, pervaded British philosophy. Improvements in telescopes had allowed people to see further, and some already conceived space as infinite. More's theory was only a short step further. Many thinkers took up More's view that space is divine, even if they left out some of his details.

For example, Cambridge philosopher Isaac Barrow is often read as following More, claiming that our conception of God's infinity involves some 'distinct Reality of Space'.[12] Barrow is another of those British philosophers who travelled a great deal because their sympathies lay on the wrong side during various parts of the English Civil War. Whilst travelling through Europe, his ship was attacked by pirates on its way to Turkey. In a Latin poem composed after the event, Barrow describes happily rebuffing the attackers.[13] (Barrow reportedly had a 'mania' for turning his thoughts into Latin verse; on returning from his travels he became ordained, and mystified the chaplain by providing 'rhyming answers' to theological questions.)[14]

Isaac Newton was taught by both More and Barrow. In the 1713 edition of his *Principia Mathematica*, Newton writes of God:

> He endures always and is present everywhere, and by existing always and everywhere he constitutes duration and space, eternity, and infinity. Since each and every particle of space is always, and each and every indivisible moment of duration is everywhere, certainly the maker and lord of all things will not be never or nowhere.[15]

A few years later, the Newtonian Samuel Clarke states:

> Space is *immense*, and *immutable*, and *eternal*; and so also is *Duration*. Yet it does not at all from hence follow, that any

thing is eternal *hors de Dieu* [outside of God]. For *Space* and *Duration* are not *hors de Dieu*, but are *caused by* and are *immediate and necessary Consequences of* His Existence.[16]

Newton and Clarke were More's most famous converts. But there were many, many others too.[17] Amongst European intellectuals, God and space were merging.

How does this new theory of space connect to mountains? People began to associate space with 'infinite' landscapes. Sand deserts. Salt flats. Ice plains. Oceans. These landscapes are not really infinite but they can appear infinite to the human eye.

Seventeenth-century philosophers connected God with space. Later thinkers connected space with infinite landscapes. Eventually, people connected God with infinite landscapes. Once this happened, infinite landscapes began to be viewed positively. Nicolson argues *this* is why mountains went from surly, burly warts to cathedrals. Although Nicolson focuses on mountains, the same evolution can be seen in other infinite-seeming landscapes. Let's take a look at writings about oceans.

Here are some of the word associations in Joseph Poole's 1657 handbook:

Sea.

Working, floating, wavie, angry, raging, swelling, licentious, curled, insulting, swallowing, awful, dreadful, toiling, pathlesse, drenching, thrift, ever-drinking, floody, ireful, stormy, surgy, ebbing, flowing, glassie, tumbling, dropsie, unbottomed, wrackful, tumultuous, aged, hoary, ruggled, ruffled, wind-hew'd, vaulting, filthy, troubled, foamy, belching, untamed.[18]

These ideas are largely negative: the sea is raging, belching, hewed by wind. Oddly, it is also 'licentious', which usually means sexually uncontrolled. James Cook would likely agree it is 'pathless'.

Around twenty years later, these descriptions of the sea as 'awful' and 'dreadful' have been turned around. Robert Boyle remarks that 'a kind of Infinity' belongs to space,[19] and later compares the infinity of God with the infinity of space. He writes that our minds cannot plumb '*the divine perfections*' or '*dimensions of space*'[20] and compares our attempts to measure space to looking at the ocean. He argues we cannot conceive the full dimensions of space, for however great we conceive them, we can always conceive them to be great. Similarly, when the eye falls upon the sea, we know that however far out to the horizon we look, our sight 'falls far short of the extent of that vast object'. Boyle now associates infinite space, and the sea, with God.

The same associations are found in Thomas Burnet, Master of the Charterhouse and a student of More. In 1681, Burnet published *Telluris Theoria Sacra (The Sacred Theory of the Earth)*. The book is a cosmography, an account of how our planet came to be. Along the way, Burnet provides a 'new' take on mountains and seas:

> The greatest objects of Nature are, methinks, the most pleasing to behold; and next to the Great Concave of the Heavens, and those boundless Regions where the Stars inhabit, there is nothing that I look upon with more pleasure than the wide Sea and the Mountains of the Earth. There is something august and stately in the Air of these things that inspires the Mind with great Thoughts and Passions; we do naturally upon such occasions think of God and his Greatness, and whatsoever hath but the shadow and appearance of INFINITE, as all things have that are too big for our comprehension, they fill and overbear the mind with their Excess, and cast it into a pleasing kind of Stupor and Admiration.[21]

Like More before him, Burnet is singing of the infinite.

Byron's *Childe Harold's Pilgrimage* (1812–16) finds God in the sea:

> There is a pleasure in the pathless woods,
> There is a rapture on the lonely shore,
> There is society where none intrudes,
> By the deep Sea, and music in its roar.

'When Byron went to the beach', writer Jonathan Raban notes, 'he mingled with the Universe.'[22] The poem by Emily Dickinson that opens this chapter expresses a similar sentiment.

Nicolson spends some time discussing the work of Joseph Addison, English essayist and co-founder of *The Spectator* magazine. Just as Burnet was a student of More's, Addison was a pupil of Burnet's. Nicolson provides several passages from Addison. Here is an excerpt from one of Addison's 1712 *Spectator* articles:

> There are none who more gratify and enlarge the imagin-
> ation, than the authors of the new philosophy, whether we
> consider their theories of the earth or heavens, the discover-
> ies they have made by glasses, or any other of their contem-
> plations on nature...when we survey the whole earth at
> once, and the several planets that lie within its neighbour-
> hood, we are filled with a pleasing astonishment, to see so
> many worlds hanging one above another, and sliding
> around the axles in such an amazing pomp and solemnity.

The main author of 'the new philosophy' Addison has in mind here is Newton, with his revolutionary theories of planetary motion. In a later article, Addison continues to muse on the bodies of our solar system. He tries to conceive how large the universe is:

> Were the Sun, which enlightens this Part of the Creation,
> with all the Host of Planetary Worlds, that move about

> him, utterly extinguished and annihilated, they would not
> be missed more than a grain of Sand upon the Sea-
> shore...There is no Question but the Universe has certain
> Bounds set to it; but when we consider that it is the Work
> of infinite Power, prompted by infinite Goodness, with an
> infinite Space to exert it self in, how can our Imagination
> set any Bounds to it?

Addison has moved from planets, to infinite space, to the infinite power of God. Nicolson argues that exactly the same connections are made with mountains. Like 'the sweep of indefinite time or the sense of infinite space', mountains are 'shadows of divinity'.

I find further confirmation of Nicolson's theory in an anonymous reply to Addison, published in a 1712 issue of *The Spectator*. The author describes themselves as someone who has taken many voyages by sea. Addison's remarks on infinity have affected them, and they write:

> This has suggested to me the reason why, of all objects that
> I have ever seen, there is none which affects my imagination
> so much as the sea, or ocean...A troubled ocean, to a man
> who sails upon it, is, I think, the biggest object that he
> can see in motion...I must confess it is impossible for me to
> survey this world of fluid matter without thinking on the
> hand that first poured it out...Such an object naturally
> raises in my thoughts the idea of an Almighty Being, and
> convinces me of his existence as much as a metaphysical
> demonstration. The imagination prompts the understand-
> ing, and, by the greatness of the sensible object, produces in
> it the idea of a being who is neither circumscribed by space
> nor time.

In the public imagination, God, space, and infinite land-scapes were becoming tangled.

Nicolson argues that Henry More laid the foundation for an 'aesthetics of the infinite'. Aesthetics is the study of beauty and art. By connecting God with space, More paved the way for Europeans to artistically appreciate vast, limitless things. Mountains and oceans are not ragged or filthy, they are God-like.

Many people read Byron and Ruskin's enthralling descriptions of mountains and, for some, reading about mountains was not enough. They wanted to see this aesthetic of the infinite for themselves. Alps tourism began in the nineteenth century, and many people journeyed to the peaks (albeit mostly people with money). Alpine clubs opened in London, Switzerland, and Germany. Slowly, a tourist infrastructure developed, birthing hill trains and mountain lodges.[23]

Robert Macfarlane's 2003 *Mountains of the Mind* describes these developments, writing that during the second half of the 1700s, people began travelling to mountains for the first time out of a spirit other than necessity. A coherent sense began to develop about the splendour of mountainous landscape. The summit of Mount Blanc was reached in 1786, and mountaineering proper came into existence in the middle of the 1800s. In part, Macfarlane explains, this was induced by a commitment to science: 'in the sport's adolescence, no respectable mountaineer would scale a peak without at the very least boiling a thermometer on the summit'. Yet it was also born of beauty. Mountains offered a complex aesthetics of ice, sunlight, rock, height, angles, and air, what John Ruskin called the 'endless perspicuity of space; the unfatigued veracity of eternal light'. To the nineteenth-century mind, these aesthetics were 'unquestionably marvellous'.[24]

Just as the mountains opened to tourists, so too did the coastlines. In the 1730s, Scarborough became the first English seaside resort. In 1738, the Prince of Wales visited Brighton, and began furnishing it with pleasure domes.

Raban blames this on Byron's Romantic Sea, which gripped the popular imagination. Every swimmer could 'wallow' in the boundless, endless sublime, and still be home 'in time for tea and muffins'.[25]

If Nicolson is correct, Byron is not the root of Europe's changing attitudes towards mountains and oceans. Instead, the root is Henry More's metaphysics of space. A poorly-known Cambridge philosopher sparked a craze for alpine tourism.

EDMUND BURKE AND SUBLIME TOURISM

Demon lanterns. The Merry Dancers. A sparking fox tail. Glimmering ice islands. The aurora borealis has been known as all these things. It occurs when the sun shoots charged particles towards Earth. The planet's magnetic poles pull them closer, and when the particles hit our atmosphere they produce light. The centre of Alaska is one of the best places to see the aurora borealis because it sits at the perfect latitude: close but not *too* close to the magnetic North Pole. I travelled into the wilderness northeast of Fairbanks with a lights-hunting trip, partly on the promise of a heated lodge to combat the subzero temperature.

We began sky watching at ten o'clock. Nothing happened for the first four hours, although the air was so clear you could see *into* space, make out dim suns behind the bright ones. We pointed at shooting stars, stamped our feet, nipped inside to warm up. Then silvery, translucent snail slime smeared across the sky.

One of the Canadians squinted at it. 'Is that a Northern Light?'

'Definitely,' said the tour guide firmly. ('See the lights!' said the adverts, 'Lights guaranteed!')

'Humph.' The Canadian was sceptical.

So was I. In *Two Old Women*, Ch'idzigyaak says the lights 'fill her with awe'. John Muir describes auroras as 'rainbow-coloured columns', silver bridges shining like raked stars, 'fused and welded and run through some celestial rolling-mill'.[1]

More minutes passed, with more feet stamping. Sluggishly the silver brightened, and flushed pea green. The group *oohed*. This was more like it. Now the aurora looked just like the photographs decorating hotel lobbies and café bathrooms throughout Alaska. I thought this display was as good as it got. I was wrong.

Someone shrieked. I turned to see more green striping the stars. Pink bars pulsed overhead and abruptly the lights were everywhere. I stumbled away from the group, face upturned. Arches lit up, crooked just so. They sketched a gothic ceiling, then a whale's ribcage. This might sound daft but I hadn't known auroras *moved*. Yet the lights scudded, fluttered, skipped. Silently. Eerily. I suspect Edmund Burke would say: sublimely.

Aesthetics is the study of beauty, but that isn't all it does. Many thinkers believe art involves other aesthetic or artistic concepts. Ugliness. Harmony. Incoherence. Philosophers of aesthetics enquire into our experiences of all these things. When I listen to Mozart, I find it beautiful. When I visit a field dotted with litter, I find it ugly. When I see a Jackson Pollock painting, I find it incoherent.

Some thinkers believe in another aesthetic concept: the sublime. The word 'sublime' is rooted in the Latin *sublimis*, 'raised' or 'uplifted'. Over the years, word meanings can drift. Today, we often use the word 'sublime' to mean 'excellent' or 'beautiful'. As one of my colleagues might say, 'That wine is sublime.' Historically though the word 'sublime' picked out a particular feeling: the feeling of *pleasurable terror*. Philosophers applied the word to the feeling, and to the things that cause the feeling. As Mary Shelley might say, 'That haunted forest is sublime.' Much of the early work on the sublime was carried out by Edmund Burke, an eighteenth-century Irish philosopher.

Ideas about the sublime have floated through philosophy for centuries.[2] What Burke's 1757 *Philosophical Enquiry into the Origin of Our Ideas of the Sublime and Beautiful* did was pull those ideas together and build on them.[3] Burke argues that although we often conflate our ideas about the 'sublime' and 'beautiful', they are very different.

For Burke, beauty is the quality of things which causes 'love, or some passion similar to it'. Beauty can be found in things of all proportions—all shapes and sizes. As Burke explains in a dryly titled chapter, 'Proportion not the cause of Beauty in Vegetables', beautiful flowers come in many forms. Besides flowers, Burke finds the following things beautiful:

- orange trees
- polished surfaces of ornamental furniture
- smooth animal furs
- swans
- smooth slopes of earth in gardens.

He mentions women's beauty in several places. This passage is almost erotic:

> Observe that part of a beautiful woman where she is perhaps the most beautiful, about the neck and breasts; the smoothness; the softness; the easy and insensible swell; the variety of the surface, which is never for the smallest space the same; the deceitful maze, through which the unsteady eye slides giddily, without knowing where to fix, or whither it is carried.

Later, Burke adds:

> An air of robustness and strength is very prejudicial to beauty. An appearance of *delicacy*, and even of fragility, is almost essential to it...

> I need here say little of the fair sex, where I believe the point will be easily allowed me. The beauty of women is considerably owing to their weakness, or delicacy, and is even enhanced by their timidity, a quality of mind analogous to it.

Burke finds women beautiful, and merely implies that men are sublime. In 1764, the German philosopher Immanuel Kant went further.

Kant is explicit that men *should* be sublime, and women *should* be beautiful. As learning is sublime rather than beautiful, women should avoid it. 'A woman who has a head full of Greek,' says Kant, 'might as well also wear a beard.'[4] (Kant blithely adds that the Italians and French feel the beautiful; and Germans, English, and Spaniards feel the sublime; yet the Dutch feel neither.) A few decades later, Mary Wollstonecraft attacked the idea that men are sublime, and women beautiful. She argues the attention paid to women's physical beauty is the 'poisoned source' of female vices, and we should prize women who inspire 'sublime emotions' through intellectual beauty.[5]

Returning to Burke, he goes on to argue that beauty involves feelings of pleasure. In contrast, the sublime involves feelings of pain and danger. Burke argues pain and danger are the most powerful human emotions, so the sublime is a strong emotion too. Anything that can produce these emotions, 'whatever is in any sort terrible', can be a source of the sublime. In the right circumstances, terrible things can give delight. Sublime feelings are produced by terrible things that are close but not *too* close.

Imagine watching an avalanche on television. The sight and sound of the tumbling snow might be gripping but you're not in mortal danger—you're not really anxious or afraid. At any time you could switch channels, or leave the room. TV can depict fearsome things but TVs are not fearsome in themselves. In this scenario, you are too far removed from the terrible thing to experience the sublime.

Now imagine you're skiing down a mountainside when an avalanche starts above you. You look up to see slabs of snow rumbling towards you. You are in mortal danger, you must escape. You definitely can't switch the avalanche off. Being in the midst of this barrage would be awful, and not at all delightful. Here, you're too close to the terrible thing for it to be sublime. To paraphrase Kant, someone who is afraid can no more judge the sublime in nature than someone who is starving can judge the beautiful in cake decorating.

Now imagine watching the avalanche begin from the balcony of a nearby chalet. You see the slabs start to slide, the shadows racing beneath them. You feel the vibrations as the snow roars downhill, hear the trees snap. You know the avalanche will miss you but you also know it has the power to destroy you. This exhibition of nature's strength is frightening and exhilarating. *This* is the right distance for the avalanche to produce feelings of the sublime.

What terrible things can produce sublime feelings? Burke suggests:

- serpents
- poisonous animals of almost all kinds
- the ocean
- mountains
- the bosom of the darkest woods
- 'howling wilderness' in the bull, lion, tiger, panther, or rhinoceros
- the raging horse

- wolves
- Stonehenge, 'those huge rude masses of stone, set on end, and piled each on other'
- caverns
- kings and commanders, their *dread majesty*
- darkness.

Mountains and oceans are, of course, central to 'aesthetics of the infinite' kindled by Henry More. For Burke, we can appreciate seas and mountains because they appear to be infinite, and because they can be sublime. A glassy sea may appear to be infinite but it's not scary, and so not sublime, whereas a storm-tossed sea can be sublime.

Burke argues all terrible things are powerful. Further, all *very* terrible things are obscure. For Burke, this is because, once we know the full extent of any danger, some of our apprehension vanishes. That is why ghosts and goblins are so scary. Burke argues no person better understood the secret of heightening terrible things than Milton. *Paradise Lost* describes Death as follows:

> The other shape,
> If shape it might be called that shape had none
> Distinguishable, in member, joint, or limb;
> Or substance might be called that shadow seemed,
> For each seemed either; black he stood as night;
> Fierce as ten furies; terrible as hell;
> And shook a deadly dart. What seemed his head
> The likeness of a kingly crown had on.

Burke praises Milton's 'gloomy pomp', his 'judicious obscurity'.

Burke concludes that our ideas of the beautiful and the sublime are very different. Unlike sources of beauty, sources of the sublime are *always* powerful, and often obscure.

Beauty is relaxing, whereas the sublime is overwhelming. Our idea of beauty is founded on pleasure, whereas our idea of the sublime is founded on pain and danger. Unlike our experience of beauty, our experience of the sublime is mixed: it involves terror *and* enjoyment.

Just as some people who read of mountains and seas wanted to see them for themselves, so some people who read of the sublime wanted to see it for themselves. European tourism to the Alps and Snowdonia increased, as did American tourism to the Niagara Falls and New Hampshire's White Mountains. From the 1860s, tourism to Australia's Jenolan Caves and New Zealand's Waitomo Caves began.

The sublime made its way into art. Figure 8.1 presents Philip James's 1803 landscape painting, *De Loutherbourg's Avalanche in the Alps*, which depicts tiny figures beside a waterfall, overshadowed by looming boulders.

Byron's 1812–18 *Childe Harold's Pilgrimage* writes of the ocean:

> ...from a boy
> I wantoned with thy breakers—they to me
> Were a delight; and if the freshening sea
> Made them a terror——'twas a pleasing fear.

The sublime is wielded to great effect in Mary Shelley's 1818 *Frankenstein*. On the way to Geneva, one character crosses a lake by boat:

> During this short voyage I saw the lightnings playing on the summit of Mont Blanc in the most beautiful figures. The storm appeared to approach rapidly; and, on landing, I ascended a low hill, that I might observe its progress. It advanced; the heavens were clouded, and I soon felt the rain coming slowly in large drops, but its violence quickly increased.
>
> I quitted my seat, and walked on, although the darkness and storm increased every minute, and the thunder burst with a

Figure 8.1 James' De Loutherbourg's *Avalanche in the Alps*

> terrific crash over my head. It was echoed from Saleve, the
> Juras, and the Alps of Savoy; vivid flashes of lightning daz-
> zled my eyes, illuminating the lake, making it appear like a
> vast sheet of fire; then for an instant everything seemed of a
> pitchy darkness, until the eye recovered itself from the pre-
> ceding flash...While I watched the tempest, so beautiful yet
> terrific, I wandered on with a hasty step. This noble war in
> the sky elevated my spirits.

In writing *Frankenstein*, Shelley made use of her early travels
through Germany and Switzerland. Later in life she published a travel book, *Rambles in Germany and Italy, in 1840,
1842, and 1843*, which includes a description of the Alps'
Splügen Pass:

> It was a dreary-looking mountain that we had to cross, by
> zigzags, at first long, and diminishing as we ascended; the
> day, too, was drear, and we were immersed in a snow-storm
> towards the summit. Naked and sublime, the mountain
> stretched out around; and dim mists, chilling blasts, and
> driving snow added to its grandeur.[6]

This would not be out of place in *Frankenstein*.

Ideas about the sublime are prominent in the wilderness
writings of John Muir. His 1894 *The Mountains of California*
describes Mount Ritter as 'sublime', a notched and weathered
'majestic mass', its glacier 'bristling' with spires, pinnacles,
and lichen-stained battlements. During a sea voyage, Muir's
1915 *Travels in Alaska* describes rough waters:

> The breakers from the deep Pacific, driven by the gale, made
> a glorious display of foam on the bald islet rocks, sending
> spray over the tops of some of them a hundred feet high
> or more in sublime, curving jags-edged and flame tinged
> sheets. The gestures of these up-springing, purple-tinged
> waves as they dashed and broke were sublime and serene,
> combing displays of graceful beautiful of motion and form
> with tremendous power.[7]

The idea of the sublime made its way into unexpected places too. The 1824 *Glasgow Mechanics' Magazine; and Annals of Philosophy* described several things as sublime, including astronomy, the hissing of auroras, and suspension bridges. Of his voyages aboard the Beagle from 1831 to 1836, Darwin wrote that the most sublime was the 'primeval forests undefaced by the hand of man'. They include the forests of Brazil, 'where the powers of Life are predominant', and those of Tierra del Fuego in Argentina, 'where Death and decay prevail'.[8] Philosophers picked out and labelled a particular kind of experience, the 'sublime', and people found things in the world that provided it.

We use the word 'sublime' less frequently now. Does that mean people are having fewer sublime experiences? I don't believe so. Many people seek to be awed *and* scared, especially through travel. For some, that is the motivation underlying caving, night scuba diving, mountain climbing.

Alain De Botton describes a trip to the Sinai desert. He finds sublime places uplifting, arguing that sublime places repeat in grand terms a lesson that ordinary life typically introduces viciously. The lesson is that the universe is mightier than we are, that we are frail and temporary and must accept limitations on our will, bow to necessities greater than ourselves. De Botton writes that this is the lesson written into the stones of the desert and the ice fields of the Poles, yet so grandly is it written there that we may come away from such places 'not crushed but inspired by what lies beyond us'.[9] Burke would agree.

Nonetheless, the twenty-first century is a different world to Burke's. Deserts. Caves. Craggy cliffs. Can we go beyond the traditional sources of the sublime?

We can. Shark diving is big business off the coasts of South Africa, Mexico, and Australia. Tourists are lowered underwater in metal cages, and use sardines to lure sharks.

The tourists get to watch the sharks eat up close, see their pink gullets and serrated teeth. Burke didn't list sharks amongst his 'howling wilderness' but he could have done. Continuing the watery theme, on the Zambian side of Victoria Falls is a natural rock formation known as Devil's Pool. At certain times of year, swimmers can perch here, just a few feet away from the rapids. You can feel the spray from relative safety.

Tornado Alley, running through Texas, Oklahoma, Kansas, and Nebraska, is seeing increased tourism. Twister tourists ride with 'storm chasers', tour companies crisscrossing the states in search of tornados. You get to see fork lightning and howling wind funnels up close. The storm photographs are stunning but chasers have died pursuing them. The website of one twister company, Silver Lining Tours, proclaims proudly that its tour packages include t-shirts.

Thinkers have long debated whether humans can create sublime things. Burke lists Stonehenge. Shelley, gliding down the Rhine, finds sublimity in tower-crowned hills, mouldering walls, and ruined castles. One historian has argued technology can be a source of the sublime, engineering marvels such as Brooklyn Bridge and Hoover Dam.[10] A philosopher has argued that skyscrapers, such as Burj Khalifa in Dubai or the Tokyo Sky Tree, are vast and powerful enough to be sublime. Skyscrapers 'overwhelm through their sheer height': we feel a sense of physical vulnerability as we imagine scaling them, or falling from their great heights.[11]

Although dams and skyscrapers can be overwhelming, I don't believe Burke would count them as sublime. Burke thought buildings could be elegant but not sublime, and I imagine this is because buildings are not scary enough. Pyramids and skyscrapers are enormous but, unlike sharks or twisters, they do not have immediate power to destroy us. Why do ruined buildings produce sublime feelings in

Mary Shelley? Not because the buildings themselves are powerful, but because they portray the destructive power of time.

Is anything manmade terrifying enough, in the right way, for Burke to accept it as sublime? Perhaps. Take our nuclear technology. 1986 saw the Chernobyl Disaster, an explosion at Ukraine's Chernobyl nuclear power plant. It released over 400 times the radiation of Hiroshima, and killed many people, quickly and slowly. Neighbouring Belarus suffered poisonous rain, crop damage, and mutated animals. The impact was also felt in Scandinavia, Switzerland, Greece, Italy, France, and the United Kingdom. As one journalist put it, the nuclear age had sent its deformed chickens home to roost.[12] Surprisingly, tourism has since grown up around the plant. Over 10,000 tourists explore it every year. The Chernobyl Tour website states, 'ABSOLUTE RADIATION SAFETY OF THE TOURISTS, granted'. Two social scientists suggest seeing Chernobyl as a 'sublime disaster'. They connect the sublime with a tourist's account of spending time around Chernobyl, how their 'sense of pleasurable excitement' became 'a sense of being overwhelmed'.[13]

Chernobyl is horrifying, and that disaster was an accident. The prospect of all-out nuclear war is chilling. Humankind has created technology capable of destroying itself, and taking chunks of the planet with it. Nuclear technology is certainly powerful enough to be sublime. Yet there has been no nuclear war. International diplomacy is anxious to prevent another nuclear bomb ever falling. Chernobyl allows tourists to feel the power of nuclear energy, to see its teeth on the buildings, safe in the knowledge that *they* are probably safe.

Are there any other sources of the sublime? Almost certainly. Burke points to very small things, including what appear to be microscopic images. Burke argues when we pursue animal life into the 'excessively small', beings that escape our senses, we trace a 'diminishing scale of existence'. We become 'amazed and confounded' at these minute wonders. Have you ever studied a drop of pond water in a microscope? Imagine doing so for the first time, and seeing that blue blob resolve into moving creatures. The existence of the microscopic world is shocking, perhaps even scary. In the twenty-first century, Timothy Morton has argued in the other direction, pointing to very large things. Morton argues 'hyperobjects', things 'massively distributed in time and space', can be sublime. Consider black holes, and their power to suck up everything, including light.[14]

Science fiction relishes imagining future sublimes. If Death Stars were real, and we could study them from a safe distance, they might elicit enjoyable horror. More recently, the 2016 film *Arrival* depicts aliens as giant octopi. The researchers communicating with the aliens are scared, and awed. *Arrival*'s director had clearly read Burke: he uses obscurity to heighten terror, clouding the alien shapes behind drifts of gas.

In the future, submarine tourism may develop further, and take us to undersea rifts or volcanos. Space ships may take us close to comets, or Jupiter's belching storms. Perhaps even close, but not too close, to black holes.

WILDERNESS PHILOSOPHY, HENRY THOREAU, AND CABIN PORN

I want to live in a cabin. Picture a timber hut, nestled in the woods or perched above a lake. A gable roof overhangs broad windows, glass reflecting the surrounding trees. Logs hunker beside the door and smoke corkscrews from the chimney.

This fantasy swam through most of my time in Alaska and, on the last day of my trip, regret crept in that it was not to be. In Fairbanks I saw pastel rectangles trumpeting 'Cabin To Rent' everywhere: pinned to the noticeboards of grocery shops, taped onto windows, tucked beside cash registers. The problem? It was April. Any cabin I rented would be an icebox. Luxury lodges, with proper insulation and heating, lay beyond my budget. I turned away from the adverts and contented myself with the *idea* of a cabin, rather than actually catching cold inside a picturesque shed. I spent most of the day writing in coffee shops and buying tacky postcards: 'Alaska—Where the Streets Are Paved with Mud!'

In hankering after cabins, I am not alone. Check out the website <https://cabinporn.com>. Or, if you're braver, search Google images for 'cabin porn'. The photos don't show sexual high jinks in log cabins, they simply show log cabins. They are usually low-built and weatherbeaten, a rustic home amongst hills or lochs or snowfields. Some look like giant crates, others are sloping organic domes, one vaunts an upturned boat for a roof. I lust after all of them, and I blame one man for it: Henry David Thoreau.

The English word 'wilderness' comes from the Old English *wildēornes*. *Wilde dēor* translates as 'wild beast', so a wilderness is a land inhabited only by wild animals. (The Old English *dēor* survives in our word 'deer'; today, we only use this for reindeer or roe deer, but it was once used for many animals.)

Humans often relate awkwardly with wilderness. Many peoples build houses, cut trees, cultivate fields, and domesticate animals. These activities transform wilderness into non-wilderness. In medieval Europe, the existence of wilderness came under threat. The Church believed areas of wilderness should be conquered, often citing Biblical grounds such as these:

> And God blessed them, and God said unto them, Be fruitful, and multiply, and replenish the earth, and subdue it: and have dominion over the fish of the sea, and over the fowl of the air, and over every living thing that moveth upon the earth. (Genesis 1:28).

Paganism, with its nature worship and sacred stones, was an enemy of Christianity. 'Woodlands,' as one historian puts it, 'were ravaged by ax-wielding monks'.[1]

In sixteenth-century Europe, the Church's power gave way to governmental power. Increasingly, states viewed landscapes as economic resources to be exploited. Agricultural techniques improved, and deforestation progressed. Philosophy didn't help. Francis Bacon deemed nature an object of scientific enquiry, to be measured and collected. Descartes saw the world as a machine, with plants and animals as queerly shaped cogs. After Newton, people conceived the whole universe as a clock.

It took a long time for more positive attitudes to wilderness to emerge in Western thought. The changes wrought by the work of Henry More and Edmund Burke played a role. Many infinite-seeming landscapes, and sources of the sublime, are wildernesses. Mountains, oceans, woods, waterfalls, and caves are rich in plants and animals. The newfound appreciation of nature fed into a nineteenth-century philosophical movement known as 'American transcendentalism'. Its label is a mouthful, and it drew on an appropriately rich alphabet soup, venerating Plato, Kant, and Samuel Taylor Coleridge. This movement sought to *understand* our relationship with nature.

Massachusetts philosopher Ralph Waldo Emerson was *the* American transcendentalist. He rose to fame through his 1836 book *Nature*.[2] It opens as follows:

> To go into solitude, a man needs to retire as much from his chamber as from society. I am not solitary whilst I read and write, though nobody is with me. But if a man would be alone, let him look at the stars. The rays that come from those heavenly worlds, will separate between him and vulgar things. One might think the atmosphere was made transparent with this design, to give man, in the heavenly bodies, the perpetual presence of the sublime.

Emerson believed people are distracted by the society around them. They would understand the world better if they spent solitary time with nature. He argues if you really *see* nature, it will bring great joy:

> In the presence of nature, a wild delight runs through man...Crossing a bare common, in snow puddles, at twilight, under a clouded sky, without having in my thoughts any

occurrence of special good fortune, I have enjoyed a perfect
exhilaration.

Emerson delights in the 'occult relation' between human
and vegetable: the fields and woods 'nod to me and I to
them'. There is no divide between nature and human consciousness. These ideas would have a huge impact on his
pupil, Thoreau.

Henry David Thoreau was born in Concord,
Massachusetts, and he never strayed far. After studying at
Harvard, he returned to Concord in 1837. There he became
friends with Emerson. At this point, Emerson was at the
height of his intellectual arc, writing and publishing his
most powerful pieces. Thoreau had read Emerson's *Nature*
whilst at Harvard, and esteemed the older man. Emerson's
journal described Thoreau with great affection: 'I delight
much in my young friend, who seems to have as free &
erect a mind as any I have ever met.'

Emerson's ideas stirred Thoreau. Emerson cherished wilderness, and often left his townhouse for nature walks.
Thoreau, cut from hardier cloth, took things further. Thoreau
travelled the wilds of New England, occasionally venturing
into Canada. He trekked and boated and climbed mountains. He described these excursions in essays titled 'A Winter
Walk' or 'A Walk to Wachusett'. Eventually, Thoreau decided
that travelling through wilderness wasn't enough. He needed
to *live* in it. Emerson disapproved, writing in his journal,
'A frog was made to live in a swamp, but a man was not
made to live in a swamp.' In turn, Thoreau's journal complains, 'I doubt if Emerson could trundle a wheel barrow
through the streets—because it would be out of character.'

Thoreau made for the wilderness regardless. In 1845,
Thoreau travelled alone into the woods, and built a cabin
by a lake known as Walden Pond. Thoreau was acting on

Emerson's philosophy, seeking understanding by spending alone time with nature.

Thoreau wanted to be a writer, as well as a nature philosopher. He took notes throughout his wilderness experience and eventually published them as *Walden; or, Life in the Woods* (see Figure 9.1).[3] Thoreau spent twenty-six months in his cabin but *Walden* condenses this into a year. The book opens as follows:

> WHEN I wrote the following pages, or rather the bulk of them, I lived alone, in the woods, a mile from any neighbour, in a house which I had built my- self, on the shore of Walden Pond, in Concord, Massachusetts, and earned my living by the labor of my hands only. I lived there two years and two months. At present I am a sojourner in civilized life again.

The book presents itself as a kind of journal. It documents Thoreau's cabin-building, fishing, and walking. More deeply, *Walden* is a work of philosophy. It's offering thoughts on how, and why, to live.

Walden opens with a long chapter titled 'Economy', on the economic forces ruling our lives. It contains one of Thoreau's most quoted lines: 'The mass of men lead lives of quiet desperation'. Thoreau is searching for an alternative to quiet desperation. His solution is simple—pioneer living.

Thoreau explains that his cabin cost $28. In a wry parody of business, he details its expenses.

Thoreau describes how he built his cabin, and then its finished appearance. He ends up with a 'tight' shingled and plastered house, ten feet wide by fifteen long. It possesses an attic and a closet, a large window on each side, two trap doors, a door at the end, and opposite a brick fireplace. Thoreau concludes, 'I thus found that the student who wishes for a shelter can obtain one for a lifetime at an expense not greater than the rent which he now pays annually.'

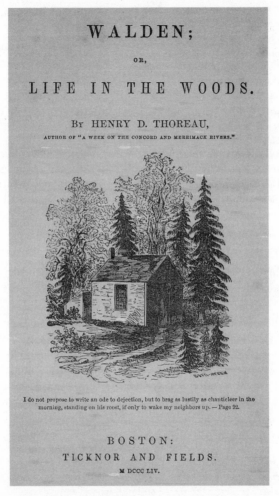

Figure 9.1 *The title page of Walden*

Boards	$8.03½
Refuse shingles for roof and sides	$4.00
Laths	$1.25
Two second-hand windows with glass	$2.43
One thousand old bricks	$4.00
Two casks of lime	$2.40
Hair	$0.31
Mantle-tree iron	$0.15
Nails	$3.90
Hinges and screws	$0.14
Latch	$0.10
Chalk	$0.01
Transportation	$1.40
In all	$28.12½

Thoreau, *Walden* (1854)

There is a note of smugness here worth pausing on. Thoreau is justly proud of his woodland life. However, he seems to assume this life is open to anyone, and that is false. Thoreau did live simply and cheaply, but he built his cabin on *Emerson's* land. Few people possess such wealthy and generous friends. Thoreau adds later he could maintain himself for a whole year by working just 'six weeks' with his hands. That may be true, but we should not underestimate the advantages Thoreau started from.

'Economy' leads to the second chapter, 'Where I Lived, and What I Lived For'. Thoreau explains:

I went to the woods because I wished to live deliberately, to front only the essential facts of life, and see if I could not learn what it had to teach, and not, when I came to die, discover that I had not lived...I wanted to live deep and suck out all the marrow of life, to live so sturdily and Spartan-like as to put to rout all that was not life.

Thoreau wanted to live to the fullest and he tried to eliminate anything that might detract from this. Like Emerson, Thoreau thought society could be a distraction.

As the chapters march on, we build up a picture of life at Walden Pond. Thoreau collects firewood, bathes, hoes, walks, and reads. Throughout the first summer, he keeps Homer's *Iliad* on his table. Thoreau watches the wildlife around him. Mice. Squirrels. Birds. In a chapter titled 'Higher Laws', Thoreau mulls the virtues of vegetarianism. He states, 'I cannot fish without falling a little in self-respect.' Sometimes Thoreau does nothing. He describes days in which he 'sat in my sunny doorway from sunrise till noon, rapt in a revery, amidst the pines and hickories and sumachs'.

My favourite passages in *Walden* are Thoreau's fussy sketches of his surroundings. Here is Walden Pond in early winter:

> The pond had in the meanwhile skimmed over in the shadiest and shallowest coves, some days or even weeks before the general freezing. The first ice is especially interesting and perfect, being hard, dark, and transparent...If you examine it closely the morning after it freezes, you find that the greater part of the bubbles, which at first appeared to be within it, are against its under surface, and that more are continually rising from the bottom; while the ice is as yet comparatively solid and dark, that is, you see the water through it. These bubbles are from an eightieth to an eighth of an inch in diameter, very clear and beautiful, and you see your face reflected in them through the ice. There may be thirty or forty of them to a square inch. There are also already within the ice narrow oblong perpendicular bubbles about half an inch long, sharp cones with the apex upward; or oftener, if the ice is quite fresh, minute spherical bubbles one directly above another, like a string of beads.

I can imagine Thoreau lying flat on the ice, jotting notes as he peers into frosty air bubbles.

Walden describes various interactions between Thoreau and other people. Visitors come to his Walden Pond, and Thoreau walks to Concord. Nonetheless, one of its underlying themes is aloneness. The chapter 'Solitude' opens as follows:

> THIS IS A delicious evening, when the whole body is one sense, and imbibes delight through every pore. I go and come with a strange liberty in Nature, a part of herself. As I walk along the stony shore of the pond in my shirt-sleeves, though it is cool as well as cloudy and windy, and I see nothing special to attract me, all the elements are unusually congenial to me. The bullfrogs trump to usher in the night, and the note of the whip-poor-will is borne on the rippling wind from over the water. Sympathy with the fluttering alder and poplar leaves almost takes away my breath; yet, like the lake, my serenity is rippled but not ruffled. These small waves raised by the evening wind are as remote from storm as the smooth reflecting surface. Though it is now dark, the mind still blows and roars in the wood, the waves still dash, and some creatures lull the rest with their notes. The repose is never complete. The wildest animals do not repose, but seek their prey now; the fox, and skunk, and rabbit, now roam the fields and woods without fear. They are Nature's watchmen—links which connect the days of animated life.

Solitude is central to *Walden*. But what exactly is it?

Philip Koch is a philosopher of solitude, and he discusses precisely this passage in Thoreau. Koch argues three features of Thoreau's evening make it solitary. First, physical isolation. Thoreau is physically alone by the pond: there are no human beings within possible sensing distance of his body. Second, social disengagement. Experientially, Thoreau is not engaged with other humans: he is not aware of anyone nearby, not searching for anyone or hiding from anyone, not longing for anyone or remembering anyone. His mind is filled with his surroundings, surroundings devoid of people. Third, reflectiveness. Although most of the passage describes a state of absorption in the sights and sounds of the evening, the last line signals a reflective distancing. Thoreau is considering symbols, such as 'Nature's Watchmen' and 'links in a chain'.[4]

Although all three of these features are present in Thoreau's experience by the pond, Koch does not believe you need all of them to be solitary. For example, Thoreau argues you can be solitary whilst surrounded by other people: 'The really diligent student in one of the crowded hives of Cambridge College is as solitary as a dervish in a desert.'

Philosophers have long praised solitude. Montaigne's *Essays* proclaim, 'The greatest thing in the world is for a man to know that he is his own.' Two centuries later, Rousseau wrote he is only 'entirely myself, and for myself' when walking alone. Why is solitude so important in *Walden*?

Thoreau's answer is that, by spending solitary time with nature, he feels at one with it:

> I go and come with a strange liberty in Nature, a part of herself...The indescribable innocence and beneficence of Nature—of sun and wind and rain, of summer and winter— such health, such cheer, they afford forever! and such sympathy have they ever with our race...Shall I not have intelligence with the earth? Am I not partly leaves and vegetable mould myself?

For Thoreau, all of us are vegetable mould.

As one Thoreau scholar points out, solitude is important to knowing nature because to know nature we must *attend* to it. We must listen to it, pay attention. That is tough when we are not alone. When we are with people, we attend to them, considering them and talking to them. In solitude, we can sink into our senses, tuning into smells, sights, and sounds.[5] Alone, Thoreau could invest hours studying the shades of Walden Pond. He could observe the movements of wood partridges, and bubbles in ice.

Emerson and Thoreau agreed humans can better understand the world through nature. Yet they disagreed over what bit of the world this would illuminate. Emerson's 1837 speech 'The American Scholar' argued that nature is the most important source of education for the scholar. This is because 'nature is the opposite of the soul, answering to it part for part'. Nature's beauty is the beauty of the scholar's own mind, and nature's laws are the laws of his own mind. Emerson argues that the precept 'Know thyself' and the precept 'Study nature' are one. Emerson is arguing knowledge of nature provides knowledge of our souls. In the end, this knowledge would show us the underlying source of nature and ourselves: the Christian God. Emerson's book *Nature* writes that sensible things have an 'unceasing reference' to spiritual nature. Nature 'lends all her pomp and riches' to religion.

Emerson is drawing on an idea found in Plato. True reality transcends the world around us, and our world is merely an imperfect shadow of it. The same idea is found in Wordsworth.

> The immeasurable height
> Of woods decaying, never to be decayed,
> The stationary blasts of waterfalls,
> And in the narrow rent at every turn
> Winds thwarting winds, bewildered and forlorn,
> The torrents shooting from the clear blue sky,
> The rocks that muttered close upon our ears,

> Black drizzling crags that spake by the way-side
> As if a voice were in them, the sick sight
> And giddy prospect of the raving stream,
> The unfettered clouds and region of the Heavens,
> Tumult and peace, the darkness and the light
> Were all like workings of one mind, the features
> Of the same face, blossoms upon one tree;
> Characters of the great Apocalypse,
> The types and symbols of Eternity,
> Of first, and last, and midst, and without end.
>
> Wordsworth, 'The Prelude' (1799)

Emerson's *Nature* opens with a quote from Plotinus, a follower of Plato: 'Nature is but an image or imitation of wisdom'. Later chapters state, 'beauty in nature is not ultimate'. Natural beauty is the 'herald of inward and eternal beauty'. Nature is an appearance, concealing the deeper reality of its creator. The objects of nature signify nature's 'hidden life and final cause'. For Emerson, natural things are symbols. 'The chaff and the wheat, weeds and plants, blight, rain, insects, sun,—it is a *sacred emblem* from the first furrow of spring to the last stack which the snow of winter overtakes in the fields.' Plants and insects are imperfect representations of something deeper, and more real.

Thoreau's early writing takes the same attitude to nature as Emerson. For example, here is Thoreau in 1843, on the summit of Wachusett:

> We could at length realise the place mountains occupy on the land, and how they come into the general scheme of the universe. When first we climb their summits and observe their lesser irregularities, we do not give credit to the comprehensive intelligence which shaped them; but when afterward we behold their outlines in the horizon, we confess

> that the hand which moulded...was privy to the plan of the
> universe.

By the time Thoreau published *Walden*, his attitude had changed. Why?

One scholar argues it is because of Thoreau's experience of Mount Ktaadn (or Katahdin).[6] Standing over 5,200 feet, this is the highest mountain in Maine, and its slopes are a stark, rocky wilderness. Thoreau moved to Walden Pond in July 1845. In August 1846, Thoreau briefly interrupted his stay to climb Mount Ktaadn. This experience tested Thoreau, physically and mentally, in a way that living in the woods had not. Walden Pond sits in gentle woodland, a few miles away from Concord. Mount Ktaadn is a brutal wilderness.

At several points, Thoreau climbed the mountain alone. He recorded the experience as follows:

> Occasionally, when the windy columns broke in to me, I caught sight of a dark, damp crag to the right or left; the mist driving ceaselessly between it and me. It reminded me of the creations of the old epic and dramatic poets, of Atlas, Vulcan, the Cyclops, and Prometheus...

> Vast, Titanic, inhuman Nature has got him [humankind] at disadvantage...She seems to say sternly, why came ye here before your time? This ground is not prepared for you. Is it not enough that I smile in the valleys? I have never made this soil for thy feet, this air for thy breathing, these rocks for thy neighbours...Shouldst thou freeze or starve, or shudder thy life away, here is no shrine, nor altar, nor any access to my ear.

On his descent, Thoreau continues to muse:

> Perhaps I most fully realised that this was primeval, untamed and forever untameable Nature, or whatever else men call it, while coming down...Nature was here something savage

and awful, though beautiful. I looked with awe at the ground I trod on, to see what the Powers had made there, the form and fashion of their work. This was that Earth of which we have heard, made out of Chaos and Old Nights...It was Matter, vast terrific...I stand in awe of my body, this matter to which I am bound has become so strange to me...I fear bodies, I tremble to meet them. What is this Titan that has possession of me? Talk of mysteries! Think of our life in nature—daily to be shown matter, to come in contact with it,—rocks, trees.

This Ktaadn experience was crucial to Thoreau's evolving philosophy of wilderness. Thoreau developed a position here that is antithetical to Emerson's.

For Emerson, nature is a route to God, it *symbolizes* a deeper reality. For Thoreau, nature is becoming 'inhuman'. There are wildernesses in which humans cannot live. Emerson wrote, 'Nature never wears a mean appearance.' In contrast, Thoreau's Nature growls, 'I have never made this soil for thy feet.'

Emerson's nature is Christian. Thoreau's nature was becoming pagan, made of 'Chaos and Old Nights'. Thoreau adds later that Mount Ktaadn is a 'place for heathenism'. He doesn't ditch God altogether but he moves towards a different kind of divinity. Thoreau's *A Week on the Concord and Merrimack Rivers*, written around the same time as *Walden*, states:

We need pray for no higher heaven than the pure senses can furnish, a *purely* sensuous life...May we not *see* God? Are we to be put off and amused in this life, as it were with a mere allegory? Is not Nature, rightly read, that of which she is commonly taken to be the symbol merely?

For Thoreau, heaven is something we can see all around us, in plants and birds and animals. Emerson's God is 'transcendent', beyond us. Thoreau's God is 'immanent', in the world around us. Thoreau wrote of Emerson, 'We do not believe in the same God.'

Thoreau also gets stuck on the mystery of *matter*. Emerson believes matter is just a gateway to the immaterial or spiritual. Thoreau comes to believe that matter is baffling. How strange is it, that our minds are 'bound' to our bodies, parcels of matter? And our bodies are continually meeting other strange parcels of matter: rocks and trees. For Thoreau, the material world is not a symbol of something deeper and more mysterious. The material world is deep and mysterious in itself.

After his trek to Ktaadn, Thoreau returned to Walden. He left the pond in 1847 but took some time to write the book which bears its name. *Walden* finally appeared in 1854. The result is a very different philosophy of nature to Emerson's. Thoreau's nature is a power in itself, and *Walden* explores humankind's relationship to nature in this light. As the novelist John Updike once wrote, 'It is the thinginess of Thoreau's prose that still excites us.' Thoreau's nature is solid, thingy, and *real*. This is quite unlike Emerson's. One scholar[7] wonders if Thoreau is trying to work past his Emersonian philosophic heritage in passages like this:

> Sometimes, after staying in a village parlor till the family had all retired, I have returned to the woods and...spent the hours of midnight fishing from a boat by moonlight, serenaded by owls and foxes, and hearing, from time to time, the creaking note of some unknown bird close at hand. These experiences were very memorable and valuable to me...It was very queer, especially in dark nights, when your thoughts had wandered to vast and cosmogonal themes in other spheres, to feel this faint jerk, which came to interrupt your dreams and link you to Nature again.

For Thoreau, nature is not abstract. Nature is what is all around us.

Having spent two years at Walden Pond, Thoreau returned to Concord. He continued to write philosophy, and was outspoken against slavery, becoming a conductor on the 'Underground Railroad', a network of secret routes and safe houses to help slaves escape into free states and Canada. Thoreau died at the modest age of forty-four, meeting death with a serenity much admired. In response to people who sought to prepare him for the afterlife, Thoreau admonished, 'One world at a time.'

On publication, *Walden* divided critics, and it continues to divide them today. Some laud Thoreau's undertaking. In 1922, poet Robert Frost wrote of Thoreau, 'In one book he surpasses everything we have had in America.' In 2004, John Updike argued that of all nineteenth-century American classics *Walden* has 'contributed most' to America's sense of itself.[8] *Walden* has even been turned into a video game.[9]

Other critics accused Thoreau of misrepresenting life at Walden Pond. Most damning was the revelation that, whilst in the woods, Thoreau's mother washed his underwear. One writer complained the 'puritanical Thoreau' was in no position to know that the mass of men lead lives of quiet desperation: 'He didn't talk to that many people. He wrote elegantly about independence and forgot to thank his mom for doing his laundry.'[10] Had he undertaken his own washing, Thoreau would not have become the first philosopher blasted for his laundry habits.

Critics dislike him for other reasons too. Bill Bryson characterizes Thoreau as 'inestimably priggish and tiresome'. In a 2015 *New Yorker* article, journalist Kathryn Schulz goes to town on *Walden*:

> The real Thoreau was, in the fullest sense of the word, self-obsessed: narcissistic, fanatical about self-control, adamant that he required nothing beyond himself to understand

and thrive in the world...Thoreau never met an appetite too innocuous to denounce. He condemned those who gathered cranberries for jam ('So butchers rake the tongues of bison out of the prairie grass') and regarded salt as 'that grossest of groceries'; if he did without it, he boasted, he could also drink less water.[11]

But like him or loathe him, Thoreau's work mattered. The philosophy of nature found in *Walden* made its way into several areas of human life. The first is wilderness conservation.

Walden is one of the founding texts of environmental philosophy. Before the nineteenth century, people felt little need for wilderness conservation. Up to then, the human population had grown slowly. It was difficult to imagine resources running out. Emerson's *Nature* adopts a medieval attitude to the natural world, writing that nature is 'made to serve'. It receives, Emerson writes, 'the dominion of man as meekly as the ass on which the Saviour rode'.

In contrast, Thoreau did not see nature as a resource we should dominate. He saw it as a valuable good that we should protect. He argues fluently for the inherent worth of living things in *The Maine Woods*:

Every creature is better alive than dead, men and moose and pine-trees, and he who understands it aright will rather preserve its life than destroy it...I have been into the lumberyard, and the carpenter's shop, and the tannery, and the lampblack-factory, and the turpentine clearing; but when at length I saw the tops of the pines waving and reflecting the light at a distance high over all the rest of the forest, I realized that the former were not the highest use of the pine. It is not their bones or hide or tallow that I love most. It is the living spirit of the tree...[which] is as immortal as I am, and perchance will go to as high a heaven, there to tower above me still.

Thoreau's journals return to this theme. For example, he worries that towns should protect their natural features, their waterfalls or meadows.

By the second half of the nineteenth century, America was beginning to think about wildlife conservation. Forests were depleted, and people were becoming aware of animal and bird extinctions. During this period, several American creatures became extinct: the sea mink, the Eastern elk, the Gull Island vole. In the twentieth century organizations formed for the protection of wildlife. Several were started by John Muir, who campaigned to protect various wilderness areas, including Yosemite Valley, California. Muir described himself as a 'disciple' of Thoreau, and kept Thoreau's portrait on his mantel. Many twenty-first-century environmental philosophers are also Thoreau converts. One soliloquizes, 'no thinker has more to offer than Henry Thoreau.'[12]

The second way *Walden* has snuck human life is through cabin porn. This phenomenon has been around for a decade, and there's even a book. *Cabin Porn: Inspiration for your Quiet Place Somewhere.*

Google is saturated with adverts for 'remote' holiday cabins and lodges. Pinterest is bursting with cabin porn. Articles on the phenomenon can be found in *The New York Times*, *The Financial Times*, and on the BBC website. Many of these reference Thoreau. Here's an example from Finn Arne Jørgensen's 2012 *Atlantic* piece, 'What It Means That Urban Hipsters Like Staring at Pictures of Cabins':

> Why can't all these people stop looking at cabins? What is the allure? Put simply, *Cabin Porn* is visual stimulation of the urge for a simpler life in beautiful surroundings. Commenters are likening it to 'channeling your inner Thoreau.' *Cabin Porn* represents the return of the homesteader, living off the grid, self-sufficient and self-reliant.[13]

For Jørgensen, cabin porn is the latest in a long tradition of dreaming about cabins, the door to a simpler life in harmony with nature. Cabin living has become shorthand for a complex set of values and aspirations, of self-reliance, doing-it-yourself, living off the land, off the grid, using our bodies in simple, honest, manual labour. All these things are supposedly lost from our modern lives of information onslaught, flashing electronics, and non-stop email. It makes us wish for a simpler time, for a simpler life. What could be simpler than living in a cabin?

Of course, for many of us, cabin porn is exactly that— porn. Even if our mothers were around to wash our laundry, most of us would shrink from a real life of *Walden*. A life without hot water, proper heating, or electricity? I would find it difficult to live that way for two weeks, let alone two years.

Although this is the case for many of us, it is not the case for all of us. This brings us to the final way *Walden* has entered human lives: wilderness travel. A big part of Alaska's allure.

In 1992, a young man named Christopher McCandless hitchhiked to the Stampede Trail. This remote track in central Alaska doesn't appear on many maps. McCandless didn't have enough food for the trail (just a ten-pound bag of rice) or waterproof hiking boots. He possessed no axe, no snowshoes, no compass. His .22 caliber rifle wasn't hefty enough to kill moose or caribou, which he would have to eat to survive. The last person to give McCandless a lift dropped him off reluctantly on a snowy track, north of Mount McKinley. McCandless smiled from the trailhead, and disappeared. From his journal, we know he survived over a hundred days in the wilderness, before succumbing to it. After McCandless' death, several books were discovered amongst his things, including *Walden*. McCandless had highlighted various passages, including this one: 'If the day and the night are such that you greet them with joy, and life emits a fragrance like flowers and sweet-scented herbs . . . that is your success. All nature is your congratulation.'

McCandless' experience was chronicled by Jon Krakauer's 1996 book *Into the Wild*, later adapted into a film. In turn, this has inspired other wilderness seekers. In 2004, Guy Grieve gave up his desk job, left his wife and sons behind, and flew to Galena, Alaska. From there he travelled deep into the woods, and built his own log cabin. Unlike McCandless, Grieve lived to tell the tale, publishing *Call of the Wild: My Escape to Alaska*.

Even if cabin living does lie in my future, it is unlikely to be a cabin I build. Nonetheless, I feel the pull of *Walden*. Thoreau asks weighty questions. What are humans? What is wilderness? How should we relate to it? His answers are equally weighty. Humans are material beings, mysterious lumps of stuff. Nature is also made of material lumps. Humans are part of nature, and we should care for its other parts.

ANCHOR LINE
GLASGOW · NEW YORK

10

IS TRAVEL A MALE CONCEPT?

A lady an explorer? A traveller in skirts?
The notion's just a trifle too seraphic.
Let them stay and mind the babies, or hem our ragged shirts:
But they mustn't, can't and shan't be geographic.

To the Royal Geographical Society,
Punch, 10 June 1893

The Lady Question. In 1890s Britain, the all-male Royal Geographical Society debated this fiercely. How far could women be involved in geography and exploration? The press ridiculed their debates, and produced the poem above. Nonetheless, the Society did not admit women fellows until 1913—twenty long years after this piece of *Punch* satire.

Over a hundred years later, Sara Wheeler's Antarctic travel book explains she had long believed the continent was 'a testing-ground for men with frozen beards to see how dead they could get'. The Frozen Beard Brigade reappear throughout *Terra Incognita*, their icy bristles embodying humanity's overwhelmingly male relationship with Antarctica.

We've seen philosophy and travel intersect repeatedly through their serpentine histories. Whether they're writing about improving our minds or the aesthetics of 'the darkest woods', philosophers have usually celebrated travel. In the twentieth century this began to change. As feminist movements gained ground, philosopher Simone de Beauvoir and others began pointing out that travel is a stereotypically *male* activity, and this poses problems. As I dug deeper into the issues surrounding travel and women, I found that travel is historically associated with men—up to and including Antarctic exploration. I also found that the Western *concept* of travel is gendered male. And that is still troublesome today.

To see why, let's step back and look at gender more generally. What is gender? Historically, people used the terms 'sex' and 'gender' interchangeably. Today, we often distinguish them. The *sex* of a person refers to their biological characteristics: their sex organs, chromosomes, and hormonal profiles. When a pregnant woman asks whether she's carrying a boy or a girl during an ultrasound, she is effectively asking after the baby's sex. The nurse might answer her by checking the foetus' sex organs on the sonograph.

In contrast, the *gender* of a person refers to the characteristics a society ascribes to men and women. As the World Health Organisation puts it:

> Gender refers to the socially constructed characteristics of women and men—such as norms, roles and relationships of and between groups of women and men. It varies from society to society and can be changed.[1]

We can illustrate this idea through examples.

Compare how British society treats women now, and how it treated them in the sixteenth century. Back then, women could not vote, enter politics, attend university, or hold positions in the army. Strict laws governed what they could and could not inherit. A pale complexion was fashionable (often attained through bleeding, or poisonous lead makeup). If I had been born in medieval England, my *sex* would be the same. But my *gender*, society's understanding of my role as a woman, would be different.

Ideas about gender vary across time and place. One of the most striking elements of Wheeler's Antarctic travels is how differently she is treated at different research bases. She describes a warm welcome at McMurdo, the US base, and notes that they have actively tried to increase the numbers of women there. In contrast, Wheeler received a stony reception at Rothera, the British base, where she is ignored and patronized by turns. Wheeler writes of her first dinner there, 'Here were British men doing what they did best: reverting to childhood and behaving like gits.' In effect, as she moved from one society to another, Wheeler's gender role shifted.

Gender is a key issue for feminist philosophy. 'Feminism' is a political movement, the quest for equality between men and women. Feminism and philosophy meet in many places: we can apply philosophy to feminist issues, and we can explore feminist issues in philosophy. One question asked by feminist philosophers is how ideas about gender can distort our worldviews. Distortions can affect our politics, our laws, what we value, and the things we pay attention to. These distortions often prove problematic for women. Here are some examples.

Theorists have long pointed out that human society is male-centred. Thoreau wrote, 'The mass of men lead lives of quiet desperation.' Albert Camus tells us, 'Man is the only creature who refuses to be what he is.' Neil Armstrong declared from the moon, 'That's one small step for a man, one giant leap for mankind.'

These people are referring to all human beings as men, and problems emerge when 'a man' is the measuring stick for 'a human'. Imagine your employer offers private medical insurance for you and your partner. It will cover you for every medical condition that could prevent you from working, *except* pregnancy and childbirth. Are these exclusions okay?

In 1976, the US Supreme Court said they were. The Court argued that, although this ruling may *appear* to discriminate against women, it doesn't really. The Court achieved this by defining the male body as the 'standard' human body. In their view, the insurance covered everything the standard human body might need (including prostate cancer and circumcision). It was acceptable not to cover things the non-standard body might need, such as pregnancy.[2] Happily, this Supreme Court decision was later overturned.

As the history of philosophy and science shows, men have long been valued more highly than women. Plato proclaims the male sex is superior to the female in 'pretty well everything', with the possible exceptions of weaving, cake baking, and cooking vegetables.[3] Aristotle characterizes females as 'mutilated' males.[4] The seventeenth-century philosopher Nicolas Malebranche described women as 'feeble-minded', 'stupid', and 'weak' (he attributes these problems to women's soggy brain fibres).[5] We have already seen Kant arguing that women should be beautiful, not sublime. He argues learning is not appropriate for women, as it will make them less attractive to the opposite sex: 'The beauties can leave Descartes' vortices rotating forever without worrying about them.' Whilst it is a 'fine thing' to teach women map reading, Kant adds women should only be taught about the *peoples* in foreign lands. 'It matters little whether or not they know the particular divisions of these countries, their industries, power, and rulers'.[6]

Hegel believed women are 'capable of education' but incapable of 'the more advanced' sciences, and philosophy. Darwin wrote that men attain to 'higher eminence' in all things than women, and 'the average of mental power in man must be above that of women'. This devaluing of women is not confined to men's thought. Margaret Cavendish laments, 'Nature...hath made men more ingenious, witty and wise than women, more strong, industrious and laborious.'

Against this backdrop, people value things associated with men more highly. For example, we associate deep voices and height with authority. One study found that CEOs with deeper voices managed larger companies and made more money. A decrease of 25 per cent in voice pitch was associated with an increase of $187,000 in annual salary.[7] Researchers have also shown that taller candidates are more likely to win elections. In 67 per cent of US presidential elections, the taller candidate won.[8] On average, men speak with lower voices than women, and are taller. Consequently, it is harder for women to be perceived as authority figures (Margaret Thatcher had elocution lessons to lower her voice, and Hilary Clinton used a customized lectern to increase her height). We associate deep voices and height with authority because we have a prior conception of men as more authoritative.

Once associations are pointed out, we can work to correct them. When appointing CEOs or presidents we should care about their ability to run companies or countries, not the pitch of their voices or how tall they stand in their socks. Feminist theorists aim to identify these kinds of associations. One way they've achieved this is by pointing out 'gendered concepts'.

A 'concept' is an idea, like blueness or democracy. Concepts are central to analytic philosophy, the movement that has dominated the English-speaking philosophical world for over a century, and stretched its tentacles beyond. Analytic philosophy is rooted in the likes of Bertrand Russell and Ludwig Wittgenstein, who emphasized the importance of 'analysing' concepts: breaking them down into parts. Working in this tradition, feminist philosophers have argued some concepts are gendered.

The basic idea is that some concepts are connected with a gender. These connections usually have long histories. For example, philosopher Charlotte Witt argues that Aristotle's concept of 'matter' is gendered female. Matter is the stuff everything is made of. Aristotle describes matter and female in many texts, such as here: 'matter yearns for form, as the female for the male and the ugly for the beautiful'. Aristotle's theory of matter underlies his views on many other subjects, including the philosophy of mind, biology, and literary theory. The problem is that, as we saw above, Aristotle believes women are inferior to men. Witt believes this negative conception of women may 'tarnish' Aristotle's entire system.[9] The Aristotelian association of matter with inferior women underlies many centuries of later thought. It explains why women were thought prone to hysteria, and unfit for higher education. This is the tradition that Malebranche, Cavendish, and Hegel inherited.

Gendering can apply to all kinds of concepts. Consider *pinkness*. Today, we associate pink with girls—and blue with boys. Despite how widespread this association is, it's fairly recent. For example, a June 1918 article from the trade publication *Earnshaw's Infants' Department* said:

> The generally accepted rule is pink for the boys, and blue for the girls. The reason is that pink, being a more decided and stronger colour, is more suitable for the boy, while blue, which is more delicate and dainty, is prettier for the girl.[10]

Although it is unclear why, this began to change in the 1940s. What is clear is that, today, the gendered association of pinkness with girls is ingrained. It would be positively idiosyncratic to dress a baby boy in pink. Pinkness is a female gendered concept.

So also is the concept of travel. The history of travel is largely a history of men. The vast majority of early travel books were authored by men: Herodotus, Homer, Zheng He, Marco Polo, Ibn Battuta, John Mandeville. Men sailed away during the Age of Exploration: Ferdinand Magellan, Francis Drake, Christopher Columbus, Jacques Cartier, Francisco Pizarro, James Cook. Grand Tourists and their bear-leaders were mostly male. As a child, I read many books about travel. *Famous Explorers. Nineteenth Century Explorers. Barrow's Boys—The Original Extreme Adventurers: A Stirring Story of Daring Fortitude and Outright Lunacy.* Women did not much feature in these tales. In a 1950 diatribe on how thoroughly the world has been explored, the Scottish writer Hilton Brown reflects on the fact women rarely travelled in the past—and adds it was a 'great advantage'.

One of the West's oldest travel books, Homer's *Odyssey*, describes Odysseus' journey home from the Trojan War. His wife Penelope waits for him there, resisting suitors who try to persuade her Odysseus is dead. Whilst Odysseus is a traveller, Penelope's role is merely to keep the hearth fires burning. Penelope's fate has dogged many other women. Women are rarely mentioned in historical travel books, and when they are they do not hold starring roles. Commonly, women are the wives of interesting men, or buxom barmaids, or prostitutes. Consider James Boswell's Grand Tour journals, Mark Twain's *Innocents Abroad*, or even Paul Theroux's *Great Railway Bazaar*.

You might be thinking that although travel history is mostly about men, there have been plenty of women travellers too. You'd be right. Jeanne Baret (1740–1807) was

> First, the official says he does not like to take the responsibility of allowing me to endanger myself in those rapids. I explain I will not hold anyone responsible but myself, and I urge that a lady has been up before, a Mme. Quinee.
>
> He says, 'Yes, that is true, but Madame had with her a husband and many men whereas I am alone and have only eight Igalwas and not Adoomas, the proper crew for the rapids, and they are away up river now with the convoy.'
>
> 'True, oh King!' I answer, 'but Madame Quinee went right up to Lestourville, whereas I only want to go sufficiently high up the rapids to get typical fish. And these Igalwas are great men at canoe work, and can go in a canoe anywhere that any mortal man can go'—this to cheer up my Igalwa interpreter—'And as for the husband, neither the Royal Geographical Society's lists, in their "Hints to Travellers" nor Messrs. Silver, in their elaborate lists of articles necessary for a traveller in tropical climates, make mention of husbands.'
>
> Mary Kingsley, *Travels in West Africa*, 1867

a member of de Bougainville's 1760s expedition. She is recognized as the first woman to have circumnavigated the world. Hester Stanhope (1776–1839) travelled through the Holy Land. Mary Wollstonecraft (1759–97) journeyed through Scandinavia in search of pirate gold. Isabella Bird (1831–1904) wandered through the United States and Asia, and became the first woman elected a fellow by the Royal Geographical Society. Mary Kingsley (1862–1900) travelled through West Africa. Gertrude Bell (1868–1926) was a spy and archaeologist who roamed through the Middle East. The Swiss explorer Isabelle Eberhardt (1877–1904) lived in, and wrote about, North Africa.

Although these women travelled, this activity was perceived to be masculine. Whilst travelling, some women found it easier to dress as men. For example, Baret joined Bougainville's ship dressed as a man, calling herself Jean rather than Jeanne. In the Syrian deserts, Stanhope eschewed riding side-saddle in favour of riding astride her horse. She adopted men's clothes, complete with pantaloons, waistcoat, turban, and sword; reportedly she shaved her hair to improve the fit of her turban. Born almost a hundred years later, Eberhardt also disguised herself as a man from an early age, enjoying the greater freedom it afforded.

At best, the non-feminine behaviour of these women was considered unusual. At worst, it was considered dangerously inappropriate, their travels 'tainted with unrespectability'.[11] To avert any suspicion of indecorum, many women travellers stressed their femininity. One way of doing so was practising acceptably ladylike pursuits whilst travelling. For example, painting occupied Marianne North, Constance Gordon Cumming, and Amelia Edwards. In her 1877 *A Thousand Miles up the Nile*, Edwards writes that the most delightful occupation in life is sketching. That said, working in Egypt poses problems:

> Everything, except the sky and the river, is yellow—yellow, that is to say, 'with a difference', yellow ranging through every gradation of orange, maize, apricot, gold, and bluff...
>
> the heat is perhaps less distressing, but the sand is maddening. It fills your hair, your eyes, your water-bottles; silts up your colour-box; dries into your skies; and reduces your Chinese white to a gritty paste the colour of salad-dressing. As for the flies, they have a morbid appetite for water-colours. They follow your wet brush along the paper, leave their legs in the yellow ochre, and plunge with avidity into every little pool of cobalt as it is mixed ready for use. Nothing disagrees with them; nothing poisons them—not even olive-green.[12]

Painting provided these women with a 'mask of decorum' over their travels.[13]

Another way women travellers emphasized their femininity was through clothes. For example, Isabella Bird notes in her 1879 *A Lady's Life in the Rocky Mountains* that her 'Hawaiian riding dress' is the 'American Lady's Mountain Dress': 'a half-fitting jacket, a skirt reaching to the ankles, and full Turkish trousers gathered into frills falling over the boots,—a thoroughly serviceable and feminine costume'. Similarly, Mary Kingsley's 1867 *Travels in West Africa* records how she was saved from death in a spike pit by her 'good thick skirt':

> Had I paid heed to the advice of many people in England, who ought to have known better, and did not do it themselves, and adopted masculine garments, I should have been spiked to the bone, and done for. Whereas, save for a good many brushes, here I was with the fulness of my skirt tucked under me, sitting on nine ebony spikes some twelve inches long, in comparative comfort, howling lustily to be hauled out.[14]

The anecdote is funny but it is no accident that it underscores Kingsley's ladylike garb.

The press and the Royal Geographical Society also reported the exploits of women travellers in ways that stressed their femininity. The subtext is that these women are feminine *despite* undertaking such masculine pursuits. As one historian explains, the emphasis placed on their womanly appearance and dress shows just how much their travelling threatened them. For all their efforts, people found it difficult to reconcile their male activities with their female gender.[15] Figure 10.1 is a 1899 cartoon of Mary Kingsley, depicted wearing a skirt and heels, *and* carrying a rifle and two cutlasses.

Figure 10.1 *Mary Kingsley*

From the 1970s, people have tried to recover the works of these women travellers. Their adventures were recounted and their travel books reprinted. The way their work is discussed conveys the sense these women were doing something forbidden or unconventional. Take these book titles:

- *Ladies on the Loose: Women Travellers of the 18th and 19th Centuries* (1981)

- *Wayward Women: A Guide to Women Travellers* (1990)

- *Unsuitable for Ladies: An Anthology of Women Travellers* (2001)

- *Women Explorers: Women Who Dare* (2007)

- *Not Just Bonnets and Bustles: Victorian Woman Travellers in Africa* (2008)

- *The Blessings of a Good Thick Skirt: Women Travellers and their World* (2010)

173

- *Women Explorers: Perils, Pistols, and Petticoats* (2012)
- *How to Climb Mt. Blanc in a Skirt: A Handbook for the Lady Adventurer* (2012)

The titles praise these women's achievements, yet hint at eccentricity. Literature scholar Susan Bassnett points out there is a comic note here that can easily be interpreted as mocking. The take-home message is that women travellers are different from other women.[16] Through their travels, these women are not acting as women.

Uncovering gendered concepts can help us see ways they have distorted our worldviews. The gendering of travel matters because we value the male concept 'travel' more highly than the female concept 'non-travel'. De Beauvoir, a great traveller herself, noticed this:

> In adventure stories it is boys who go around the world, travel as sailors on boats, subsist on breadfruit in the jungle. All important events happen because of men. Reality confirms these novels and legends. If the little girl reads the newspapers, if she listens to adult conversation, she notices that today, as in the past, men lead the world. The heads of state, generals, explorers, musicians and painters she admires are men.[17]

Men sail boats, survive in the jungle, explore new lands. We know these things are valuable and important because they are the subjects of newspaper articles, history books, and novels. In contrast, women stay at home, keep house, raise children. These things are rarely the subjects of newspapers or histories, so they do not appear to be as valuable or important. Women are not doing exciting things—they are simply the sisters, wives, and daughters of people who are.

Although philosophy is concerned with gendered concepts in general, it has not said much on the gendering of

174

travel in particular. However, outside of philosophy, several theorists have studied it. One writes that in many societies being feminine has been defined as sticking close to home. Masculinity, by contrast, has been the passport for travel.[18] Because traditionally men have travelled and women have not, another scholar describes travel as a 'gendering' activity.[19] Literature theorists flag the way adventure travel books such as *Robinson Crusoe* are aimed at young boys. These books reinforce patriarchal values, on which men are deemed superior.[20]

The male gendering of travel is problematic in many ways. One reason is that, historically, it has obstructed women from travel. Thomas 'the Travailer' Palmer argued female travellers should be prohibited, except in very special cases. Another reason is that even though women have been travelling in great numbers since the mid twentieth century, their travels often go unrecognized and uncelebrated. Consider these landmark books on travel and its history. Fussell's 1980 *Abroad*. Eric J. Leed's 1991 *The Mind of the Traveller*. De Botton's 2002 *The Art of Travel*. Women travellers are largely absent.

Today, lists of the 'most important' or 'most famous' travellers and explorers are still monopolized by men. A 2006 *Wunderlust* article on the '10 Greatest Travellers of All Time' found nine to be male.[21] The Royal Geographical Society's 2010 *Explorers: Tales of Endurance and Exploration* lists fifty-nine individual explorers, fifty-six of whom are male. Collins' 2016 *Explorers: Fascinating Facts* covers forty-five explorers, of whom forty-two are male. In 2011, expeditioner. com produced a list titled 'The 30 Greatest Travellers of All Time'.[22] This article is especially notable because it actually lists more animal travellers than women travellers. Kira Salak and Sylvia Earle are outnumbered by Cat Videos, the Arctic Tern, and the African Wildebeest.

Just as women's travels go unrecognized, so does their travel writing. Men dominated travel writing into the 1970s[23] and the problems are still unresolved. In a 2017 *Matador* article, travel writer Carrie Speaking[24] points out that male authors prevail in lists such the *The Telegraph*'s 'The 20 Best Travel Books of All Time'.[25] She notes that the annual *Best American Travel Writing* anthologies include few female writers and, of the seventeen volumes published to date, women edited less than a third—yet 'Bill Bryson and Paul Theroux each got to do it twice'.

'Travel' is not the only concept that is gendered male. 'Philosophy' is also deeply associated with maleness. Ask someone on the street to name a philosopher and almost everyone will name a man. Confucius, Plato, Descartes, Wittgenstein, Heidegger. Joshua Poole's 1657 handbook for poets provides a list of words associated with 'Philosopher'. Alongside 'sage' and 'contemplative' it includes 'bearded'.[26] Unsurprisingly, this has led to problems in academic philosophy, including the underrepresentation of women.[27] Many other male-dominated fields suffer similar issues.

Nonetheless, there is plenty of light on the horizon. In travel, and in philosophy, work is underway to break down male stereotypes. Scholarship is growing on travellers such as Gertrude Bell and Isabella Bird, and on philosophers such as Anne Conway and Mary Astell. We are also seeing increasing numbers of articles with titles such as 'Ten Inspiring Female Travellers.'[28] Greater awareness of these women will chip away at beardyness.

11

THE ETHICS OF DOOM TOURISM

> Perhaps it's my natural pessimism, but it seems that an awfully large part of travel these days is to see things while you still can.
>
> Bill Bryson, *Down Under* (2000)

When we travel to a place, we travel at a certain time. Travelling to the States in 2020 would be very different to a trip in 1920 (or even 2120). Places change, and sometimes they are erased from the map altogether. Fighting destroyed the Porcelain Tower of Nanjing during the 1850s. In 1982 a Brazilian hydroelectric project submerged the world's most powerful waterfall, Guaira Falls, under an artificial lake. I backpacked around Syria in 2005, gawking at Aleppo's Umayyad mosque and the ruins of Palmyra. Through war, these majestic sites have now been partially destroyed.

Tourist spots have always come in and out of existence. Yet there is a growing feeling that places will soon be winking out of existence *en masse*, because of climate change. This has led to a sharp increase in 'doom tourism'. Travellers are rushing to see the Maldives before the sea submerges them, and the Columbia Icefield before it melts. Tourists don't want to miss their 'last chance' to see these places.

Alaska is already facing climate change. Warm winters are causing the permafrost layers to melt, and the sea ice to retreat.[1] Have you heard the legend, 'Eskimos have fifty words for snow'? The legend is problematic, not least because the Arctic has many native peoples, with many different languages.[2] Nonetheless, there is some truth in it. For example, the Yupik people of western Alaska have many different words for sea ice. Yet researchers have found that some of these words, such as *tagneghneq* (thick, dark, weathered ice), are becoming obsolete.[3]

I didn't travel to Alaska because of last chance worries, but I did once travel to Antarctica with them in mind. When I was little, I inhaled stories about Antarctic explorers. Ernest Shackleton. Roald Amundsen. Apsley Cherry-Garrard. When I was older, I feared that if I didn't see the white continent in its pristine state soon I might miss my shot.

'Last chance to see' tourism has been around for a long time. In 1989, thousands of tourists travelled to Germany to witness the 'last' of the Berlin wall before it fell.[4] Yet the past few years have seen a sharp rise in this kind of tourism, and this is connected with growing awareness about climate change.

The Earth has undergone cycles of warming and cooling throughout its history but there is scientific consensus that its recent, accelerated period of warming is our doing.[5] Burning fossil fuels like oil and coal has released carbon dioxide and other gases into the atmosphere. Think of the atmosphere as a kind of blanket around the planet, trapping the sun's heat. When the blanket gets thicker, less heat escapes, leading to a warmer Earth. Scientists estimate the planet is warming ten times faster than on its usual cooling–warming cycle.

As a result of the Earth's temperature rise, many of its features are changing. With few exceptions, glaciers around the world are retreating. (Leaving behind them, as naturalist John Muir once put it, hollows like the tracks of 'travelling animals'.) The northern regions of the world are seeing less snow cover, and less permafrost. The oceans are warming, and some sea creatures cannot survive the warmth. This has led to the 'bleaching' and death of coral reefs. 2016 saw another huge swathe of Australia's Great Barrier Reef killed off.[6] At the Poles, ice sheets and sea ice are melting, leading to rises in the planet's sea levels. Parts of the Kiribati islands are already underwater, and a project is underway to relocate its citizens to Fiji.[7] The last ten years have seen a global sea level rise of 4 centimetres. Scientific projections estimate the level could rise by as much as 2 metres over the next century. Even a 0.5 metre rise would be hugely problematic for coastal regions such as the Maldives, the Seychelles, the Solomon Islands, Micronesia, the Netherlands, and southern Florida.

The growing consciousness that these places are at risk has led to an increased drive to visit them. 'Doom tourism' is not the only label for this phenomenon. It has also been called 'catastrophe tourism', 'last chance to see tourism', 'extinction tourism', and even 'climate change voyeurism'.[8] These worries drove Douglas Adams and Mark Carwardine's 1990 book *Last Chance to See*. The writer and zoologist travelled to exotic locations aiming to find species on the brink of extinction, including Indonesian Komodo dragons and Chinese Yangtze river dolphins.

A 2014 *Time* article, '10 Amazing Places to Visit before They Vanish', featured Montana's Glacier National Park and the Seychelles.[9] A 2016 *Rough Guide* article, '20 Destinations to See before They Disappear', included Brazil's rainforests, Tanzania's Kilimanjaro, and Argentina's ice fields. A 2016 article in *Condé Nast Traveller* explains that global warming is the reason for the disappearances of these places in its title.[10]

The Effects of Global Warming: 12 Places That Are Disappearing

. . . .

1 The Dead Sea
2 The Alps
3 The Great Barrier Reef
4 The Amazon
5 Venice
6 The Rhone Valley
7 Key West
8 The Maldives
9 Alaska
10 Napa Valley
11 Mumbai
12 Glacier National Park

Condé Nast Traveller, 2016

What is the ethical problem of doom tourism? Ethics is the branch of philosophy dealing with morality, with right and wrong. Some human actions, such as theft and murder, are generally deemed *wrong*. Other actions, such as nursing the sick and giving to charity, are generally deemed *right*. In itself, there's nothing unethical about the practice of doom tourism. If a tide is about to sweep away a sand castle, why not run to the beach to catch a last glimpse?

The problem is that the act of visiting 'at-risk' places may hasten their demise. Coral reef tourists may accidentally whack the creatures, or leave rubbish and sunscreen residue in the water. By feeding fish, tourists can change their behaviour. Arctic tourists are concentrated in particular areas, and large numbers can trample delicate vegetation. Boat and helicopter noises disturb the wildlife, and trash doesn't break down in freezing temperatures.

At-risk places are sometimes so remote they require huge fuel expenditures, by plane or train or boat. Polar cruises are especially unkind to the environment, producing high carbon dioxide emissions per person per trip.[11] Over the last decade, this problem has become known as the 'paradox' of doom tourism. Tourists are hurrying to visit a place before it's gone, yet this very activity is contributing to the place's destruction. If the act of visiting at-risk sites puts them at further risk, it may not be ethical to visit them.

We usually believe it is immoral to destroy things that have value. It is wrong to murder, because human lives are valuable. It is wrong to destroy art museums, because artworks are valuable. If glaciers or coral reefs are valuable, it would be wrong to hasten their demise.

Why might we think at-risk places are valuable? Environmental ethics is concerned with precisely these kinds of questions. It offers two kinds of answers. One answer is, these places are valuable *to humans*. The Kiribati islanders need their islands to live on. Polluting the landscape is bad for our health. Destroying coral reefs destroys creatures we find beautiful.[12]

Another answer is, these places are valuable *in themselves*. The well-being of animals and plants matters, regardless of how useful they are to humans. We should value the richness and diversity of non-human life for its own sake.[13] These claims are usually made about animals and plants but we can extend them to inanimate landscapes. Glaciers and coastal regions are also rich and diverse, and we should also value them. This is the position of Henry Thoreau and John Muir.

Many at-risk places are valuable to humans. We all need clean land to live on, to grow food, and source water. I also believe these places are valuable in themselves. If you think they are valuable in *any* way, then the right thing to do is protect them. As these places are being damaged by tourism, it looks as though the best way to guard them is to stop tourism. That would halt the damage caused by human visitors, and slow their destruction.

Yet some thinkers have argued we shouldn't stop doom tourism, because the positive consequences of tourism outweigh the negative. Although tourism may accelerate the demise of at-risk places, it may also safeguard them. We could achieve this by creating 'tourist ambassadors' for at-risk places.

A political ambassador represents their country abroad, promoting its national interests. Similarly, a tourist ambassador represents an at-risk place, spreading the word about how valuable and fragile it is. Political ambassadors are intimately familiar with their country, and tourist ambassadors are personally familiar with their at-risk places. The International Association of Antarctica Tour Operators aims 'To create a corps of ambassadors for the continued protection of Antarctica by offering the opportunity to experience the continent first hand'. This familiarity allows them to develop an emotional bond. Sara Wheeler has become one such ambassador for Antarctica.[14]

In principle, the plan to create tourist ambassadors is sensible. Antarctic tourists would be awed by the continent's beauty and unique ecosystems, and they would return home with a better understanding of how to protect it. They might tell their loved ones about the Antarctic Treaty, which currently preserves Antarctica for peaceful and scientific purposes. They might discuss ways of combatting climate change more generally. Given this plan, it would be ethically acceptable to allow tourism to continue.

The problem with the plan is that it doesn't seem to work. Several studies have shown that, despite high hopes, doom tourists do *not* become tourist ambassadors. A 2010 study found no evidence that Antarctic tourists returned with greater environmental awareness.[15] A 2014 study found that, after returning from Antarctica, in some respects tourists moved towards *less* ecologically friendly beliefs. Further, they had barely increased their knowledge of Antarctic animals. This study concluded, 'Tourists returning from the Antarctic do not seem to play the role of ambassadors because many visitors merely want a last chance to glimpse a vanishing world.'[16] A 2016 study found that around 70 per cent of Great Barrier Reef tourists were motivated to see it before it disappears. However, there was a 'strong disassociation' between tourists' concern for the reef, and the damage their own visits might cause.[17]

In light of this evidence, tourists have two ethical options available. First, quit tourism to at-risk places altogether. Second, continue tourism to at-risk places, but try harder to travel responsibly. There are many projects enabling people to offset their carbon footprints, like tree planting.[18] In addition, tour companies and individual tourists could work harder at educating everyone about endangered places.

In my view, further education about at-risk places could benefit tourists in unexpected ways. Some philosophers have argued that increased *knowledge* about a landscape brings increased *pleasure*. This line of thought can be applied to doom tourism.

We have already met 'aesthetics', the area of philosophy that considers beauty and art. 'Environmental aesthetics' considers a particular kind of beauty: the beauty of the natural world. Allen Carlson works in this field, and he compares our appreciation of manmade artworks with our appreciation of nature.[19] Whilst in New York, I visited the Museum of Modern Art. I was especially keen to see Van Gogh's *Starry Night*. As I approached the oil painting,

I understood *what* I should appreciate. I studied the painted canvas, not the frame or the surrounding wall. I also understood *how* I should appreciate it. I looked at *Starry Night*, and didn't listen to it, smell it, or taste it.

In contrast, it is less obvious what we should appreciate in nature, or how. Carlson considers various answers, modelled on our appreciation of artworks. Perhaps we should appreciate a hilly landscape the same way we appreciate a Van Gogh painting, by standing still and admiring the view. However, Carlson argues this doesn't work. Unlike a painting, the hills are not two-dimensional, or static, or a representation of something else. Carlson argues if we admire hills the same way we admire a painting, we are missing what the hills are. We don't just *see* a hilly landscape. We also smell the heather, hear the wind, prick our legs on the gorse bushes. Humans design paintings to fit on a canvas, to lead the eye in specific ways. In contrast, natural environments don't have frames or focal points.

Yet, Carlson argues, this doesn't mean there aren't better or worse ways to appreciate nature. A solid knowledge of art's history and traditions can help us to better appreciate paintings: to 'look for contours in the Florentine school and for colour in a Bonnard'. Similarly, a solid knowledge of nature helps us better appreciate natural environments. We can find that knowledge in science.

When I passed through Denali Park, I saw a blur of greens spreading out every which way. Had a botanist been beside me, their experience would have been different. They would have seen willows and alders, and distinguished spruce from birch trees. The botanist would perceive and understand the peeling trunks and twisted leaf shapes.

Carlson would argue the botanist's aesthetic experience would be better than mine. The botanist's greater knowledge would allow them to perceive the park more richly, and pick out significant features of the landscape. They would know what is worth appreciating. Just as the art critic and art historian are 'well equipped' to appreciate the beauty of art, the naturalist and ecologist are well equipped to appreciate the beauty of nature.

If this argument is right, then learning about the geology or wildlife of Antarctica isn't just worthwhile for Antarctica. Turning tourists into ambassadors is a benefit but not the only one. It's also worthwhile for the tourists, because that knowledge will allow us to appreciate the continent's beauty in new and enriched ways.

Looking ahead, if our attempts at protecting places like Antarctica or the Great Barrier Reef fail, these sites will continue to deteriorate. Unfortunately, as their at-risk status increases, so too may visitor numbers. Conversely, if we succeed in protecting these places, they may cease to be at-risk. That could lead to visitor numbers dropping.

Climate change is going to affect all of us, but it's hitting some places earlier than others. Take the inhabitants of Shishmaref, an Alaskan island village north of the Bering Strait. In 2002 they voted to relocate to the mainland because, without ruinously expensive flood defences, their island cannot cope with the climate-change-induced erosion. Unfortunately, as the relocation programme is also expensive, it has not yet taken place.[20] Meanwhile, in 2016 the US government granted relocation moneys to residents of the Isle de Jean Charles, Louisiana. Their island is sinking into the sea.[21] Climate change refugees are emerging within US borders; yet, in 2017, the US president arguably implied the phenomenon is a hoax.[22]

Many of the problems we've looked at in this book are still debated today. We still worry about the nature of maps, the best way to conduct science, and what the ideas of peoples unfamiliar to us mean for innatism. Yet as the twenty-first century advances into the looming shadow of climate change, the kind of ethical problems discussed here may come to overshadow all other issues in the philosophy of travel.

VENISE ET LE LIDO

12

WILL SPACE TRAVEL SHOW THE EARTH IS INSIGNIFICANT?

The human figure itself takes on immense majesty when you meet it solitary in a landscape that scarcely speaks of humanity at all...The smallness and the weakness of the human creature is there made unmistakably apparent...This is a true feeling, presenting humanity as it is, amid the antiqiuity, the size and grandeur of the earth. It is worth a long hard journey to attain it.

Freya Stark, 'Remote Places' (1950)

I landed in Amsterdam with a suitcase of curiosities. Alaskan 'Moosetard' Mustard. *Qiviuq*, muskox under-wool. King Salmon Jerky. I would give most of them away but I planned on keeping the birch syrup—it would go well with Dutch pancakes.

At Schiphol Airport the border guard was polite and ruggedly handsome. (All Dutch border guards are ruggedly handsome—perhaps they are rounded up throughout the country to meet clandestine job criteria.)

'Good evening,' he said in that softly clipped accent. 'What is your purpose in entering the Netherlands?'

'*Goedenavond. Ik woon in Groningen.*' My Dutch is poor but I can manage that much.

He blinked. 'You live in Groningen?'

'*Ja.*'

'Okay then.' The guard folded my boarding pass into my passport and slid it back through the hatch. With a nod of sympathy, he added, '*Goede treinreis.*'

He was wishing me a good train journey. Groningen is only two hours north of Amsterdam, yet to the Dutch it is the icy hinterland.

'*Dank je,*' I replied ruefully, although the hinterland was really not so far.

I couldn't work on the train home—brain too soupy with sleep. Instead I watched the scenery skimming past the window. Inky fields against an inky sky. Miles of rectangles striped with irrigation ditches. There is so *much* world. I'd seen fragments of Alaska, and I was returning to a city whose centre could generously be said to cover two square miles. In between, I'd flown over 4,000 miles of planet. And that's just our planet. It's another 238,900 miles to the moon. Depending on where Earth is in its orbit, it's around 140 million miles to Mars. We only touch a fraction of what's out there, and understand less than that. Looking forwards and upwards, I wondered what philosophy can say about these depths—what can it say about space travel?

Travelling can change the way we feel about our home places. Before voyaging abroad, you might believe your home town to be the most beautiful, most important place in the world. It is unlikely you will feel that way on your return. In this vein, Socrates once quelled a wealthy land-owner by showing him that his 'great' estate cannot be found on a world map. Grand Tour bear master Richard Lassels remarks that travelling takes noblemen down a few notches in their pride, for they see how small their lands and countries are. Novelist Gustave Flaubert agrees that travelling makes you modest: 'You see what a tiny place you occupy in the world.' By showing how large the world is, travel reveals how small our home places are.

Of course, the size of a thing need not mean we value it less. It's true that sometimes we value larger things more than small ones. Larger houses are usually more expensive than smaller houses. A double hamburger costs more than a single. Yet there is no necessary connection between size and value. Small things can be just as valuable as large ones. Imagine Van Gogh had painted a series of miniature landscapes. Each canvas glows with colour, yet measures just one inch square. We would value these miniatures just as highly as Van Gogh's other paintings, if not more highly, for their intricacy.

Similarly, take the Lilliputians described in *Gulliver's Travels*, shown in Figure 12.1. Gulliver portrays these people as miniature humans, standing around six inches tall. The Lilliputians live in little houses, and work in little towns. Like us, each Lilliputian is a thinking, feeling being. If they really existed, I believe we would and should value their lives as highly as our own. We value children's lives as highly as adults' lives, the lives of slim or short people as much as those of plump or tall people. During an evacuation, nobody shouts, 'Large people first!'

So, the size of a thing need not affect its value. A painting can be beautiful regardless of its size, and a person's life is valuable whether they are a giant or a Lilliputian. In 1951, Bertrand Russell made precisely this point:

> There is no reason to worship mere size. We do not necessarily respect a fat man more than a thin man. Sir Isaac Newton was very much smaller than a hippopotamus, but we do not on that account value him less.[1]

Figure 12.1 *Gulliver and the Lilliputians*

If there is no connection between size and value, the size of your home place should not devalue it. The problem is, when we come to realize how small our home places are, our attitudes towards them often change. What is going on?

We can answer this question using Guy Kahane's distinction between *value* and *significance*. Kahane argues that, to be significant, something needs to have value. However, merely having value isn't enough to be significant. Significance also requires importance, in the sense that something merits our attention and concern. He explains:

> Seen alongside the horrific (or the wonderful), many things become simply insignificant—worthy of no attention at all. If you witness a terrible tragedy, it would be inappropriate to obsess about a stain on your suit. After spending a week attending to soldiers injured and disfigured in the civil war, Whitman wrote to his mother that '...really nothing we call trouble seems worth talking about.'[2]

To give another example, consider Van Gogh's painting of a cherry blossom. This painting has intrinsic value as a beautiful artwork. Imagine you are looking at this painting in Amsterdam's Van Gogh Museum, alongside many of his other paintings. An art critic might say this particular painting is *somewhat* important, as a milestone in Van Gogh's artistic development. Now imagine that his other paintings were all destroyed. This blossom painting would become *momentously* important, as the last remaining example of Van Gogh's work.

The idea is that the intrinsic value of a thing is unchangeable, but its significance can change. The aesthetic value of a Van Gogh painting remains the same no matter what. Yet, if the painting became the last of its kind, its significance would increase.

One way the significance of a thing can change is by placing it in a larger geographical context. Think about the stories that make it into local, national, and international newspapers. An architecture prize awarded to a new building in Groningen might make the front page of local newspaper, *Dagblad van het Noorden* (literally, *The Daily of the North*). Groningen buildings do not often win architecture prizes, so the news item is significant within this context. In contrast, the prize might merit a brief notice in a Dutch national newspaper, and receive no mention at all in the *New York Times*. No matter how *valuable* a new meringue-shaped restaurant may be, its *significance* decreases the farther one you get from Groningen. That's because it has been placed in a wider context: across the Netherlands, and across the world, many buildings win architecture prizes.

This shift in the significance of things is what we become conscious of when we travel. Regardless of how charming your home place is, its significance reduces the further away you get from it. That's because you place your home town in a larger context. If I stayed on my train all the way to its final destination, I would arrive at Leeuwarden. This is a miniature jewel of a city, flaunting a medieval centre looped by canals, crowned by a leaning bell tower. Within the northern Netherlands, Leeuwarden is extremely significant, a historic and graceful state capital. However, its significance pales the farther away you get. By European standards, Leeuwarden is relatively insignificant: it is one of a thousand medieval cities. This is why travel makes you modest. Although your home place retains its value no matter how far you travel, you become conscious of its insignificance.

If travelling from Fairbanks to Amsterdam can induce a feeling of insignificance, what might space travel do?

As novelist Douglas Adams once wrote in his *Hitchhikers Guide to the Galaxy*, 'Space is big, really really big...'.

I said above that the Earth lies 140 million miles from Mars. Our nearest stars, the Alpha Centauri system, are 4 light years away—that's around 25 trillion miles. Our galaxy, the Milky Way, contains anywhere from 100 to 400 billion stars. Scientists estimate that the observable universe is around 93 billion light years across. The whole universe is at least 250 times as large as the observable universe, and it may be infinite.[3] Our brains weren't built to comprehend these numbers.

Philosophy and science fiction are littered with remarks connecting the size of the universe with human insignificance. As Adams puts it:

Far out in the uncharted backwaters of the unfashionable end of the western spiral arm of the Galaxy lies a small unregarded yellow sun. Orbiting this at a distance of roughly ninety-two million miles is an utterly insignificant little blue-green planet.

Such sentiments go back a long time.

In antiquity, the philosopher Cicero authored a short story on this theme. *The Dream of Scipio* describes how a Roman general, Scipio Aemilanus, travels to a 'place on high, full of stars, and bright and shining'.[4] Whilst watching the Milky Way, 'the surpassing whiteness of its glowing light', Scipio writes:

And as I surveyed them from this point, all the other heavenly bodies appeared to be glorious and wonderful,—now the stars were such as we have never seen from this earth; and such was the magnitude of them all as we have never dreamed; and the least of them all was that planet, which farthest from the heavenly sphere and nearest to our earth, was shining with borrowed light, but the spheres of the stars

> easily surpassed the earth in magnitude—already the earth
> itself appeared to me so small, that it grieved me to think
> of our empire, with which we cover but a point, as it were, of
> its surface.

Scipio is seeing how small our planet is, and how the great
Roman Empire is even smaller than this. Observing Scipio,
his grandfather tells him:

> I see...that you are even now regarding the abode and
> habitation of mankind. And if this appears to you as insig-
> nificant as it really is, you will always look up to these
> celestial things and you won't worry about those of men.
> For what renown among men, or what glory worth the seek-
> ing, can you acquire?

This is a thought experiment. In asking us to imagine inter-
stellar space travel, Cicero is asking us to reconsider the
significance of our lives.

In his *Pensées* (literally, *Thoughts*), the French philosopher Blaise Pascal writes:

> When I consider the short duration of my life, swallowed up
> in the eternity before and after, the little space which I fill,
> and can even see, engulfed in the infinite immensity of
> spaces of which I am ignorant, and which know me not,
> I am frightened.

The eternal silence of these infinite spaces frightens lots
of us.[5]

Many thinkers are awed by the littleness of humans and
our planet. When we reflect on the immensity of the universe, should we conclude that humankind and Earth are
insignificant?

Russell considers this question. He writes that although
we find the minute size of humankind in the astronomical abyss 'bewildering and oppressive', our reaction is
not rational. As he believes we should not worship size,

Russell claims to stand unimpressed by the depths of space and time.[6]

Kahane develops Russell's position into a larger argument. Kahane argues that although there is something embarrassingly megalomaniac in the desire for grand cosmic significance, this desire might be fulfilled. Kahane's reasoning runs as follows.

Humans value human life highly. Many humans also value plant and animal life highly. We pour time and money into wildlife conservation, protecting nature reserves, defending areas of natural beauty. In contrast, we rarely place such a high value on inanimate things, such as clouds or tables. Kahane imagines an asteroid strike that destroyed all life on Earth, yet created a magnificent series of craters. Kahane writes that few people would think this a 'marked improvement'. This suggests we value life more highly than non-life.

Suppose we are right to value life more highly, that plants and animals really do have a higher intrinsic value than non-living things. This would mean our planet is valuable *and* significant within the context of our solar system. The sun, the moon, Mars, and Jupiter are impressive. But they are merely clumps of rock and gas. We would be small, yet we would maintain our importance. And the significance of Earth may not stop there.

Kahane argues if there is extraterrestrial life on other planets, the significance of Earth may decrease. In the same way that Groningen's significance decreases in the context of other European cities, our planet would be less important if it were merely one of many living planets. Yet, if our planet is the *only* living planet in the universe, it would be of gigantic cosmic significant. As Kahane writes:

> When we are impressed by our tiny size, by the vastness of the space that envelopes us, and conclude that we must be very unimportant, this may be because we forget to consider

> just how empty this immensity is. An observer might take a
> very long time to find us in this immensity, but besides us,
> he might find in it little or nothing to care about.[7]

If we are alone in the universe, the importance of our little blue-green planet may outweigh its size. Our home planet might be tiny *and* the most significant thing in the entire universe.

I don't know whether there is life on other planets. That's a question for astronomers and biologists. I do know that, whether there are or aren't extra-terrestrial creatures, philosophy offers tools for thinking about humanity's place in the universe. Just as Scipio's worries about the Roman Empire abated, our worries may abate too.

I was still troubled by my impending move away from Groningen. Once the train arrived I beeped my travel card and wheeled my luggage out onto the station concourse, standing amid the swoops of concrete facing the main streets. It was almost midnight and the scent of wet leaves hung in the air. I breathed in the night, tasting the canal under the rain, and began to walk home. The art museum loomed to my right, neon cubism run amok. Cobbles glistened. My suitcase humped over the uneven pavements. The city was old and solid, and it made me feel reassuringly small. Its rambling history yawned far before me and would stretch long after me. I was home.

RETURNING HOME

Top 10 Vintage Tips

1. On pain of death, avoid returning corrupted

On the observer's return, Plato tells us he will report to a council of the state where, if he is thought to have become 'appreciably better', he will be rewarded with higher recognition. However, if it seems to the council that the observer has 'returned corrupted', he must talk to no one 'young or old' and live as a private person; if convicted of meddling in some educational or legal question, '*he must die*'.

Plato, *Republic* (c.380BCE)

2. After foreign travel, consider space travel

'Tis also one fruit of travelling, that by seeing variety of places and people, of humours, fashions and forms of living, it frees us, by degrees, from that pedantry and littleness of Spirit, whereby we are apt to censure every thing for absurd and ridiculous, that is not according to our own way, and the mode of our own Country; But if instead of crossing the Seas, we could waft our selves over to our neighbouring Planets, we should meet with such varieties there, both in Nature and Mankind, as would very much enlarge our thoughts and Souls, and help to cure those diseases of little minds.

Thomas Burnet, *The Theory of the Earth* (1684)

3. Leave behind foreign fashions

When he comes out of those forranie countries, he likewise come out of their humours and habits, and come home to himself, fashioned to such carriage in his apparel, gesture, & conversation, as in his own country most plausible, and be approved.

Robert Dallington, *A Method for Travell* (1605)

4. Serve your country

On returning home, the traveller shall 'reap contentment, honour, and estimation'. However, to achieve this, the traveller must undertake several offices. He must manifest 'unto all men his uncorrupt and unspotted Religion'. He must banish 'all affectations, and apish tricks, and fashions of other nations', if they are not better than our own. Additionally, he must act as his conscience dictates with regard to matters affecting 'Honour, Wealth, or Revenge'. Most importantly, he must serve God, the Prince and the Commonwealth.

Thomas 'the Travailer' Palmer, *An Essay of the Means how to make our Trauailes, into forraine Countries, the more profitable and honourable* (1606)

5. Ensure you have not travelled too long

I had already given enough time to languages and likewise to reading the works of the ancients, both their histories and their fables. For conversing with those of past centuries is much the same as travelling. It is good to know something of the customs of various peoples, so that we may judge our own more soundly and not think that everything contrary to our own ways is ridiculous and irrational, as those who have seen nothing of the world ordinarily do. But one who spends too much time travelling eventually becomes a stranger in his own country.

Descartes, *Discourse on the Method* (1637)

6. Do not bore people with travel talk

Some 'degenerate' travellers do not manage this: 'all their talks is still Forraine...*magnifiying* other Nations, and *derogating* from their own'. You can't exchange more than three words with them before they are at the 'other side of the Sea', commending the 'Wines of France' or the 'fruits of Italy'. Worse yet are those who have evidently been 'Abroad under hot Climates' through their *diseases*.

James Howell, *Instructions for Forreine Travell* (1642)

7. Know that your country is best

France was a good Country to ride through, Italy a good Country to look upon, Spain a good Country to understand, but England a good Country to live in. So wishing the traveller a prosperous Voyage, I here cast Anchor.

Edward Leigh, *Three Diatribes* (1671)

8. Pack up camp carefully

- 'complete' your collections of plants and rocks
- make careful drawings of your encampment
- make presents of your travelling gear to attendants, as they will be 'mere litter' in England
- arrange your 'memoranda', indexing journals if necessary
- have your instruments 'verified' on their return, so that we know their readings were accurate

- recalculate your observations, sending a copy by post to England
- draw up lithograph maps, to aid future travellers.

Francis Galton, *The Art of Travel* (1855)

9. After train journeys, handle luggage and ladies

- the 'disposal' of ladies should speedily remove them from the 'noise, bustle, and confusion inseparably attendant on the arrival of the train'
- collect your luggage quickly. If your luggage is found at the Railway Clearing House, and your identity can be ascertained, the property will be forwarded 'on the payment of a fine of 6*d*. for each article'
- If you will later be returning to the station, you should 'observe the relative position of the station in connection with the other buildings by which it is surrounded', so as to reach it again without difficulty.

Anon, *The Railway Traveller's Handy Book* (1862)

10. And, finally, return home

We shall not cease from exploration,
And the end of all our exploring
Will be to arrive where we started
And know the place for the first time.

T. S. Eliot, 'Little Gidding' (1942)

ACKNOWLEDGEMENTS

A great many people have contributed to this project, from the philosophers who offered travel anecdotes at conferences, to the friends and family who listened to me witter on about Locke and elephants. I owe special thanks to Felix Ringel, Cathy Thomas, Matthew Duncombe, Erin Wilson, Chris Cowie, Doina-Cristina Rusu, Julian Baggini, Aaron Garrett, Simon James, Katharine Jenkins, Sue James, Jeremy Dunham, Kathy Puddifoot, Eleanor Rosamund Barraclough, Andy Cooper, David Faraci, and David Strahan. I am also grateful to Sophie Scard at United Agents, and to the Oxford University Press team—especially Peter Momtchiloff, Luciana O'Flaherty, and three anonymous referees. This is a better book for all of you.

NOTES

CHAPTER 1. WHY DO PHILOSOPHERS CARE ABOUT TRAVEL?

1. On mountain roaming, see Leed (1991: 58–9); on the wisest heroes, see Strabo (1917: I.30).
2. I quote from the 1845 edition of Montaigne's works.
3. Maillart (1950: 121).
4. <https://www.lonelyplanet.com/travel-tips-and-articles/how-to-go-off-the-grid-when-you-travel/40625c8c-8a11-5710-a052-1479d276568e>.
5. Howell (repr. 1869: 74).
6. Descartes (1984: I.113–16).
7. Russell (2009: 67).
8. See Berkeley (1713: Preface) and Hume (1739: 457–8; 467). For more travel-philosophy metaphors, see van Den Abbeele (1991) and Winkler (2004).
9. Fussell (1980: 38–41).
10. See Bohls and Duncan (2005: xvi–xvii) and Thompson (2011: 13–23).
11. Bryson (1989: 187).
12. Rousseau (1921) and Mill (2015: 71).
13. Maillart (1950: 115).

CHAPTER 2. WHAT ARE MAPS? BRIAN HARLEY ON CARTOGRAPHIC DECEPTION

1. Monteith (1866: 16).
2. <https://www.popsugar.co.uk/smart-living/Map-Tattoos-41902743#photo-41902743>.

3. Andrews (1996) compiles 321 definitions of maps, drawn from the year 1649 onwards. For example, Nathan Bailey's 1730 *Dictionarium Britannicum* defines a map as, 'A plain figure, representing the several parts of the surface of the earth...or it is a projection of the surface of the globe, or part thereof.' Skipping forward a few hundred years, Barbara Taylor's 1992 *Maps and Mapping* characterizes maps as 'Flat drawings of the world seen from above'.

4. Anon, cited in Churchill (1704: lxxvi).

5. Harley (1989: 6).

6. Harley himself points to a discussion of the Official State Highway Map of North Carolina in Wood and Fels (1986). The same themes are tackled in Woods's 1992 *The Power of Maps* and Monmonier's 1996 *How to Lie with Maps*.

7. <https://www.regjeringen.no/en/aktuelt/the-high-north-top-of-the-world-top-of-t/id420872/>.

8. <https://www.dur.ac.uk/ibru/news/boundary_news/?itemno=21759>.

9. <http://www.bbc.co.uk/news/uk-politics-37337175>.

10. <http://www.nytimes.com/1988/09/03/world/soviet-aide-admits-maps-were-faked-for-50-years.html>.

11. Kitchin and Dodge (2007). For commentary, see Fernández and Buchroithner (2014) and Rose-Redwood (2015).

12. Take <https://www.OpenStreetMap.org>, a wiki platform created in 2004. This online mapping project is continually being built by a community of mappers. Using Global Positioning System (GPS) devices, volunteer mappers contribute and maintain data about roads, trails, cafés, and railway stations all over the world. These new forms of mapping are especially important in countries such as Peru, that lack civilian mapping agencies. See Gerlach (2015).

13. See Peterson (2003: 1–2).

14. Wood (1992: 30–1) discusses Tolkien's map-making process but argues it is 'not often the case' that maps grow or develop. I wonder if Wood would reconsider this view, in light of online maps.

15. Blundeville (1589: To the Reader).

16. See Bishop (2014) and Olds (2005).
17. See Dodge and Perkins (2015) and (1987).

CHAPTER 3. FRANCIS BACON ON THE PHILOSOPHY OF SCIENCE AND FROZEN CHICKEN

1. Whewell (1834: 59).
2. Bacon (1964: 97).
3. Bacon (1900:144).
4. Bacon (1900: 372–81).
5. Seller (1670: 12).
6. For example, Aristotle credits the Egyptian 'priestly caste' with founding the mathematical arts (*Metaphysics* 1.981b23–4). For further discussion of the Egyptian origins of Greek philosophy, see Coetzee and Roux (2005: 5).
7. Bacon (1964: 131–2).
8. For more on the theology underlying Bacon's work, see McKnight (2006).
9. Bacon (repr. 1874: 550).
10. Wood and Kolek (2010: 95–6).
11. Boyle (1665–6).
12. Leigh (1671: 7–9).
13. Palmer (1606: 1–17).
14. Darwin (1859: Preface).
15. I borrow these from Carey (1997), who provides more information on travel and the Royal Society generally.
16. Anon, cited in Churchill (1704: lxxiii).
17. Swann (2001: 23–4).
18. Bacon (1900: 359).
19. Boyle (1772: I:303).
20. Bacon (1900: 367).
21. Cited in Leed (1991: 192).
22. Wollstonecraft (1889).
23. You can even visit it virtually. See <http://news.national-geographic.com/2015/05/150520-infinity-cave-son-doong-vietnam-virtual-tour-photography-conservation/>.

24. <https://www.theguardian.com/environment/2009/feb/24/antarctica-mountains>.
25. <https://www.theguardian.com/world/2014/aug/01/amazon-tribe-makes-first-contact-with-outside-world>.
26. <http://www.scientificamerican.com/article/just-how-little-do-we-know-about-the-ocean-floor/>.

CHAPTER 4. INNATE IDEAS IN DESCARTES, LOCKE, AND CANNIBALS

1. For a native Alaskan perspective on the purchase, see Worl (2016: 305–8).
2. For more on Montaigne's influence over Descartes, see Foglia (2014: §6).
3. Descartes (1984: I.115).
4. Clarke's (2006) excellent biography gives more information on Descartes' drifting travels (p. 37–8); on his 'wanderlust' (p. 93–5); and on his death (p. 405–10).
5. Borrowed from Clarke (2006).
6. Descartes (1984: I.118–19). For a rare discussion of this passage, see Perkins (2014: 25–6).
7. Descartes (1984: II.31–5).
8. Locke (1984: 279). I have updated some of Locke's spelling.
9. Locke (1690: I.1.2).
10. Locke (1858: 252–3).
11. On Locke's travel books, correspondence, and notes, see Carey (2005: 23–7) and Talbot (2010).
12. The essay was likely authored by Locke or Edmond Halley; see Wolfe (2014: 147). In my view, the essay's hyperbolic style is unlike Locke's.
13. See Anon, cited in Churchill (1704: lxxiii).
14. See Talbot (2010: 9–14).
15. See Carey (2005: 14–23).
16. Boyle (1665–1666: 188).
17. Talbot (2010: 209–10).

18. For more on Locke's relationship with Bacon, Boyle, and the Royal Society with regard to travel, see Carey (2005), Talbot (2010), and Anstey (2011).

19. See Connolly (2013).

20. This and later references are taken from Locke (1690: I.II.3–I. III.9).

21. <http://articles.latimes.com/2013/jan/15/world/la-fg-india-mercy-killings-20130116>.

22. Locke (1699: 447).

23. Locke (1699: 449).

24. Smith (2015) provides a book-length study of developing views about human racial difference during the modern period. Locke himself participated in the slave trade; see Glausser (1990). Winkler (2004) addresses racism and nationalism in Locke and other British empiricists, within a broader discussion of their attitudes towards multiculturalism.

25. Mbiti (1969: 2). For more on religion in African culture, see Oladipo (2004).

26. See Anderson (2005: 131–2).

27. The objections can be found in Stillingfleet (1697: 89–90). On the ways that other philosophers replied to Locke, including the third Earl of Shaftesbury and Francis Hutcheson, see Carey (2005). For more on this particular controversy, see Talbot (2010: 161–77).

28. Lee (1702: 25).

29. Moore (1973: 121).

30. For example, see the readings collected in the first chapter of Coetzee and Roux (2005).

31. Locke (1699: 496–7).

32. See Chomsky (1965).

33. The classic study is Berlin and Kay (1969). Interestingly, the term 'grue' is borrowed from a philosophical article on a different issue entirely; see Goodman (1955).

34. <http://www.japantimes.co.jp/life/2013/02/25/language/the-japanese-traffic-light-blues-stop-on-red-go-on-what/#. WT-6xsbMy34>.

35. See Everett (2005).
36. See Haviland (1998).

CHAPTER 5. WHY DID TOURISM START? SEX, EDUCATION, AND THE GRAND TOUR

1. <https://www.alaskacenters.gov/explore/culture/history>.
2. On this historical trading, see the previous source and also <https://phys.org/news/2016-06-world-metals-alaska-coast-hundreds.html>.
3. For more on those early encounters, see Worl (2016: 303–5).
4. <https://www.canadiangeographic.ca/article/reverse-colonialism-how-inuit-conquered-vikings>.
5. Coryate (1905: 236).
6. Strachan (2013).
7. Black (2011: 1).
8. Bacon (1996: 364–6).
9. Newton (2008: 9–11).
10. Nugent (1749: I.vii–viii).
11. Rousseau (1921: 374).
12. Rousseau (1921: 418).
13. Smith (1776: 357).
14. Lassels (1670: xiii–xxxvii).
15. Boulton and McLoughlin (2012: 155).
16. See Moulton (2000: 113–18) and Littlewood (2001: 40–52).
17. See Moulton (2000: 171).
18. Thicknesse (1770: 158).
19. Cited in Littlewood (2001).
20. Recorded in Black (2011: 83).
21. Black (2011: 76).
22. Littlewood (2001: 107–9).
23. Thicknesse (1778: 118–25).
24. Cavendish (1663: 71–4).
25. Wollstonecraft (1989: VII.300–1).
26. Thompson (2007: 38–9).
27. Lever (1873).
28. <https://ourworldindata.org/tourism>.

29. See Relph (1976).
30. Shopping abroad also has a long history. See <http://www. transitionsabroad.com/listings/travel/articles/women-travel- in-history.shtml>.
31. De Botton (2003: 113).
32. Camus (1963: 13–15).
33. <http://www.nytimes.com/2011/04/03/travel/03Cover. html?_r=0>.
34. Blanton (1997: 2).
35. Norman Douglas, quoted in Fussell (1987: 15).
36. <http://www.prospectmagazine.co.uk/columns/travel-the- last-great-wilderness>.
37. See Whitaker (1981–2: 161).

CHAPTER 6. TRAVEL WRITING, THOUGHT EXPERIMENTS, AND MARGARET CAVENDISH'S *BLAZING WORLD*

1. Lopez (2014: 282).
2. Marshall (2016: 245; 264).
3. Invented by Foot (1967).
4. Although I do know that how you answer will depend on which ethical system you favour. For example, a 'utilitarian', seeking to maximize the greatest number of happy people, *would* flip the switch. In contrast, a 'Kantian' would *not* flip the switch, arguing that the lone person should not be used as a means to an end (in this case, saving five other people).
5. For more on thought experiments in philosophy and other disciplines, see Sorensen (1999) and Ierodiakonou and Soux (2011).
6. On the history of North Pole, Alaska, see <http://www. northpolealaska.com/community>.
7. Hayden (2012: 15) has more on this.
8. More (1998: 61).
9. I quote from the 1659 edition of *New Atlantis*.
10. Pugliese (2006).
11. I quote from the 2015 edition of *Blazing World*.

12. Pepys (2000: VIII.163).
13. I owe these biographical details to Whitaker (2002).
14. Cited in Hakluyt (1889: XII.66). I have updated some of Willes's spelling.
15. Taken from explorer Luke Foxe (1635).
16. For more on these ideas, see Cottegnies (2010). On the hunt for the Northwest Passage more generally, see Waters (1958).
17. Cavendish (1663: 137).
18. Cavendish (1663: 243–5).
19. It should be remembered that Bacon died in 1626. So, although the Royal Society took themselves to be following through on Baconian principles, Bacon himself could not make any pronouncements about Hooke's *Micrographia*.
20. This and the preceding passages are taken from Cavendish (2001: 50–3).
21. (Locke, 1690: II.xxiii.11).
22. See Cottegnies (2010).
23. This and the preceding passages are taken from Cavendish (2001: 50–3).

CHAPTER 7. MOUNTAIN TRAVEL AND HENRY MORE'S PHILOSOPHY OF SPACE

1. Ransom (1940: 551).
2. Amongst other achievements, Nicolson became the first woman appointed full professor at an Ivy League, when she joined Columbia in 1941. I use the (1959) edition of *Mountain Gloom, Mountain Glory*.
3. Poole (1657: 129).
4. Berkeley (repr. 2013: 109; 140).
5. Ghica (1858: 324).
6. Muir (1915: 152–3).
7. For more detail on these theories, see Thomas (2018).
8. Descartes (1984: I.227–8).
9. More (1878: 91).
10. The diagram is borrowed from Dainton (2010: 2).
11. More (1995: 52–60).

12. Barrow (1734: 171).
13. Barrow (1859: IX.458–80).
14. On Barrow's mania, see Overton (1885: 302). On his ordination, see Feingold (2007).
15. Newton (1999: 941).
16. Clarke (1717: 129–31).
17. For details, see Thomas (2018).
18. Poole (1657: 179).
19. Boyle (1999–2000: VIII.269).
20. Boyle (1999–2000: IX.389).
21. Burnet (1684, 139–40).
22. Raban (1992, 14).
23. For an accessible introduction to the history of tourism, see <http://ieg-ego.eu/en/threads/europe-on-the-road/the-history-of-tourism#TheBoominMassTourisminthe19thCentury>.
24. Macfarlane (2003: 15–16).
25. Raban (1992: 10–14).

CHAPTER 8. EDMUND BURKE AND SUBLIME TOURISM

1. Muir (1915: 315–16).
2. Brady (2013) provides an excellent history of the sublime, before and after Burke.
3. I quote from the (1990) edition.
4. Kant (2011: 35–7).
5. Wollstonecraft (1793: 53–4).
6. Shelley (1844: 59).
7. Muir (1915: 273).
8. Darwin (2008: 506).
9. De Botton (2003: 169).
10. Nye (1994).
11. Brady (2013: 119; 142–7).
12. <http://www.telegraph.co.uk/travel/destinations/europe/ukraine/articles/how-can-i-visit-chernobyl-and-is-it-safe/>.
13. Goatcher and Brunsden (2011).
14. Morton (2013: 1).

CHAPTER 9. WILDERNESS PHILOSOPHY, HENRY THOREAU, AND CABIN PORN

1. Oelschlaeger (1991: 72).
2. I quote from the 1836 edition of *Nature*.
3. I quote from the 2004 edition of *Walden*.
4. Koch (1997: 13–14).
5. Cafaro (2004: 111–14).
6. Oelschlaeger (1991: 145–51).
7. Cafaro (2004: 116).
8. <https://www.theguardian.com/books/2004/jun/26/classics>.
9. <https://www.waldengame.com>.
10. See Garrison Keillor, cited here: <https://newrepublic.com/article/123162/everybody-hates-henry-david-thoreau>.
11. <http://www.newyorker.com/magazine/2015/10/19/pond-scum>.
12. Cafaro (2004: 139).
13. <https://www.theatlantic.com/technology/archive/2012/03/what-it-means-that-urban-hipsters-like-staring-at-pictures-of-cabins/254495/>.

CHAPTER 10. IS TRAVEL A MALE CONCEPT?

1. <http://www.who.int/gender-equity-rights/understanding/gender-definition/en/>.
2. See Bem (1993: 74–6).
3. Plato (*Republic*: 455c).
4. Aristotle (*Generation of Animals*: 737a28).
5. Malebranche (1997: 279; 326).
6. Kant (2011: 35–8).
7. Mayew et al. (2013).
8. <https://www.psychologytoday.com/blog/caveman-politics/201210/it-s-weird-candidate-height-matters-in-elections>.
9. See Witt (1998).

10. <http://www.smithsonianmag.com/arts-culture/when-did-girls-start-wearing-pink-1370097/#2sj34VwxoPMgmERc.99>.
11. Enloe (2014: 40).
12. Edwards (1888: 310).
13. Birkett (1989: 108).
14. Kingsley (2003: 270).
15. See Birkett (1989) and Wolff (1992).
16. Bassnett (2005: 226).
17. de Beauvoir (1949: 351).
18. Enloe (2014: 21).
19. Leed (1991: 90).
20. Thompson (2011: 169–70).
21. <http://www.independent.co.uk/travel/news-and-advice/the-10-greatest-travellers-of-all-time-6104262.html>.
22. <www.theexpeditioner.com/2011/12/19/the-30-greatest-travelers-of-all-time/>.
23. See Hulme (2005: 89–90) and Bassnett (2005).
24. <https://matadornetwork.com/life/travel-writing-genderized-heres-needs-change/>.
25. <www.telegraph.co.uk/travel/galleries/The-20-best-travel-books-of-all-time/>.
26. Poole (1657: 155).
27. <https://www.bpa.ac.uk/uploads/2011/02/BPA_Report_Women_In_Philosophy.pdf>.
28. This is a particularly good one: <http://www.huffingtonpost.co.uk/alice-nettleingham/inspirational-female-travellers_b_9405484.html>.

CHAPTER 11. THE ETHICS
OF DOOM TOURISM

1. <https://climatechange.alaska.gov>.
2. It originated in the work of anthropologist Franz Boas (1911). For a recent, accessible overview of the debate (controversial itself), see <https://www.newscientist.com/article/mg21628962.800-are-there-really-50-eskimo-words-for-snow/>.

3. <https://www.theguardian.com/environment/2016/dec/19/alaska-sea-ice-vanishing-climate-change-indigenous-people>.
4. See Dawson et al. (2011: 254).
5. <https://climate.nasa.gov/evidence/>.
6. <http://edition.cnn.com/2016/11/28/asia/great-barrier-reef-coral-death/>.
7. <http://uk.businessinsider.com/islands-threatened-by-climate-change-2012–10?r=US&IR=T/#kiribati-1>.
8. See Eijgelaar et al. (2010) and Dawson et al. (2011).
9. < http://time.com/42294/amazing-places-visit-vanish/>.
10. <http://www.cntraveler.com/gallery/10-places-to-visit-before-theyre-lost-to-climate-change>.
11. Eijgelaar et al. (2010).
12. A classic and accessible text expressing this kind of view is Passmore (1974).
13. These claims are drawn from a list composed by Naess and Sessions; see Naess (1986).
14. <http://www.wanderlust.co.uk/magazine/articles/interviews/sara-wheeler-interview?page=all>.
15. Eijgelaar et al. (2010).
16. Vila et al. (2016).
17. Piggott-McKellar and McNamara (2016).
18. <http://www.carbonfootprint.com and http://www.world-landtrust.org/eco-services/offsetting/individuals>.
19. Carlson (1979).
20. <https://www.theguardian.com/us-news/2016/aug/18/alaska-shishmaref-vote-move-coastal-erosion-rising-sea-levels>.
21. <https://www.nytimes.com/2016/05/03/us/resettling-the-first-american-climate-refugees.html?_r=0>.
22. <https://www.nytimes.com/2017/06/02/us/politics/climate-change-trump-hoax-scott-pruitt.html>.

CHAPTER 12. WILL SPACE TRAVEL SHOW THE EARTH IS INSIGNIFICANT?

1. Russell (2009: 270).
2. Kahane (2014: 750).

3. <http://www.bbc.co.uk/earth/story/20160610-it-took-centuries-but-we-now-know-the-size-of-the-universe>.
4. I quote from the (1883) translation.
5. Pascal (2003: 61).
6. Russell (2009: 370).
7. See Kahane (2014: 753).

CREDITS

Pictures

Credits

PUBLISHER'S ACKNOWLEDGEMENTS

We are grateful for permission to include the following copyright material in this book.

Extract from *West with the Night* by Beryl Markham reprinted by permission of Pollinger Limited (www.pollingerlimited.com) on behalf of the Estate of Beryl Markham.

Excerpt from Bill Bryson *Down Under* (2000), reproduced with permission from Bill Bryson.

Excerpt from Freya Stark 'Remote Places' (1950). All rights reserved.

The publisher and author apologize for any errors or omissions in the above lists. If contacted they will be pleased to rectify these at the earliest opportunity.

SELECT BIBLIOGRAPHY

Adams, Douglas (2016). *The Hitchhiker's Guide to the Galaxy.* Pan: London.

Anderson, E. A. (2005). *Everyone Eats: Understanding Food and Culture.* New York University Press: New York.

Andrews, J. H. (1996). 'What Was a *Map?' Cartographica* 33: 1–11.

Anstey, Peter (2011). *Locke and Natural Philosophy.* Oxford University Press: Oxford.

Aristotle (1984). *The Complete Works of* Aristotle. Edited by Jonathan Barnes. Princeton University Press: Princeton, NJ.

Bacon, Francis (1659). *The New Atlantis. A Work unfinished.* London.

Bacon, Francis (1874). *The Letters and the Life of Francis Bacon Including All His Occasional Works, Vol. VII.* Edited by James Spedding. Longmans, Green, Reader, and Dyer: London.

Bacon, Francis (1900). *The Works of Francis Bacon, Vol. VIII: Translations.* Houghton Mifflin: Boston.

Bacon, Francis (1964). *The Philosophy of Francis Bacon: An Essay on its Development from 1603 to 1609 with New Translations of Fundamental Texts.* Edited by B. Farrington. University of Chicago Press: Chicago.

Bacon, Francis (1996). *Francis Bacon.* Edited by Brian Vickers. Oxford University Press: Oxford.

Barrow, Isaac (1734). *The Usefulness of Mathematical Learning Explained and Demonstrated.* Translated by John Kirkby. Stephen Austin: London.

Barrow, Isaac (1859). *The Theological Works of Isaac Barrow.* Edited by Alexander Napier. Cambridge University Press: Cambridge.

Bassnett, Susan (2005). 'Travel Writing and Gender', in *The Cambridge Companion to Travel Writing,* pp. 225–41. Edited by

Peter Hulme and Tim Youngs. Cambridge University Press: Cambridge.

Bem, Sandra L. (1993). *The Lenses of Gender.* Yale University Press: New Haven.

Berkeley, George (1713). *Three Dialogues between Hylas and Philonous.* London.

Berkeley, George (2013). *The Correspondence of George Berkeley.* Cambridge University Press: Cambridge.

Berlin, Brent and Paul Kay (1969). *Basic Color Terms: Their Universality and Evolution.* University of California Press: Berkeley.

Birkett, Dea (1989). *Spinsters Abroad: Victorian Lady Explorers.* Basil Blackwell: Oxford.

Bishop, Elizabeth (2014). *Complete Poems.* Chatto & Windus: London.

Black, Jeremy (2011). *The British and The Grand Tour.* Routledge: Beckenham.

Blanton, Casey (1997). *Travel Writing: The Self and the World.* Twayne Publishers: New York.

Blundeville, Thomas (1589). *A Brief Description of Universal Maps & cards and of their use.* London.

Boas, Franz. (1911). *Handbook of American Indian languages.* Government Printing Office: Washington.

Bohls, Elizabeth and Ian Duncan (2005). 'Introduction', in *Travel Writing 1700–1830: An Anthology,* pp. xiii–xxvii. Edited by Elizabeth Bohls and Ian Duncan. Oxford University Press: Oxford.

Boulton, James T. and T.O. McLoughlin (2012). *News from Abroad: Letters Written by British Travellers on the Grand Tour, 1728–71.* Oxford University Press: Oxford.

Boyle, Robert (1665–1666). 'General Heads for a Natural History of a Countrey, Great or Small, Imparted Likewise by Mr. Boyle', *Philosophical Transactions* 1: 186–9.

Boyle, Robert (1772). 'Certain Physiological Essays and Other Tracts' in *The Works of the Honourable Robert Boyle, Vol. I.* London.

Boyle, Robert (1999–2000). *The Works of Robert Boyle.* Edited by Michael Hunter and Edward B. Davis. Pickering and Chatto: London.

Brady, Emily (2013). *The Sublime in Modern Philosophy: Aesthetics, Ethics, and Nature.* Cambridge University Press: Cambridge.

Bryson, Bill (1989). *The Lost Continent: Travels in Small Town America.* Harper & Row: New York.

Bryson, Bill (2010). *Notes from a Big Country.* Transworld Publishers: London.

Burke, Edmond (1990). *Philosophical Enquiry into the Origin of our Ideas of the Sublime and Beautiful.* Edited by Adam Phillips. Oxford University Press: Oxford.

Burnet, Thomas (1684). *The Theory of the Earth, Vol. I.* London.

Byron, George (1812/1829). *Childe Harold's Pilgrimage.* Du Jardin-Sailly Brothers: Brussels.

Cafaro, Philip (2004). *Thoreau's Living Ethics: Walden and Pursuit of Virtue.* University of Georgia Press: Athens, GA.

Camus, Albert (1963). *Notebooks: 1935–1942.* Translated by Philip Thody. Harvest/HBJ Book: New York.

Carey, Daniel (1997). 'Compiling Nature's History: Travellers and Travel Narratives in the Early Royal Society', *Annals of Science* 54: 269–92.

Carey, Daniel (2005). *Locke, Shaftesbury, and Hutcheson: Contesting Diversity in the Enlightenment and Beyond.* Cambridge University Press: Cambridge.

Carlson, Allen (1979). 'Appreciation and the Natural Environment', *The Journal of Aesthetics and Art Criticism* 37: 267–75.

Cavendish, Margaret (1663). *Orations of Divers Sorts.* London.

Cavendish, Margaret (2001). *Observations upon Experimental Philosophy.* Edited by Eileen O'Neill. Cambridge University Press: Cambridge.

Cavendish, Margaret (2015). *The Description of a New World, Called The Blazing-World.* CreateSpace Independent Publishing Platform: United States.

Chomsky, N. (1965). *Aspects of a Theory of Syntax.* The MIT Press: Cambridge, MA.

Churchill, Awnsham (ed.) (1704). *A Collection of Voyages and Travels, Vol. I.* London.

Cicero, Marcus Tullius (1883). *Somnium Scipionis, the dream of Scipio Africanus Minor, being the epilogue of Cicero's treatise on polity.* Translated by W. D. Pearman. Deighton, Bell & Co: Cambridge.

Clarke, Samuel (1717). *A Collection of Papers, Which passed between the late Learned Mr. Leibniz and Dr. Clarke, In the Years 1715 and 1716*. Edited by Samuel Clarke. London.

Clarke, Desmond M. (2006). *Descartes: A Biography*. Cambridge University Press: Cambridge.

Coetzee, P. H. and A. P. J. Roux (2005). *The African Philosophy Reader*. Routledge: London.

Coleridge, Samuel Taylor (1997). *The Complete Poems of Samuel Taylor Coleridge*. Penguin: London.

Connolly, Patrick (2013). 'Travel Literature, the New World, and Locke on Species', *Society and Politics* 7: 103–16.

Coryat (rep. 1905). *Coryat's crudities: hastily gobled up in five moneths travells in France, Savoy, Italy, Rhetia commonly called the Grisons country, Helvetia alias Switzerland, some parts of high Germany and the Netherlands*. J. MacLehose and Sons: Glasgow.

Cottegnies, Line (2010). 'Utopia, Millenarianism, and the Baconian Programme of Margaret Cavendish's The Blazing World (1666)', in *New Worlds Reflected: Travel and Utopia in the Early Modern Period*. Edited by Chloë Houston. Routledge: Aldershot.

Dainton, Barry (2010). *Time and Space*. Acumen Publishing Ltd: Stocksfield.

Darwin, Charles (1859). *On the Origin of Species*. John Murray: London.

Darwin, Charles (1958). *The Autobiography of Charles Darwin 1809–1882*. Edited by Nora Barlow. Collins: London.

Darwin, Charles (2008). *The Voyage of the Beagle*. Cosimo Classics: New York.

Dawson, J., M. J. Johnston, E. J. Stewart, C. J. Lemieux, R. H. Lemelin, P. T. Maher, and B. S. R. Grimwood (2011). 'Ethical Considerations of Last Chance Tourism', *Journal of Ecotourism* 10: 250–65.

de Beauvoir, Simone (1949). *The Second Sex*. Translated by Constance Borde and Shelia Malovany-Chevallier. Vintage Books: New York.

De Botton, Alain (2003). *The Art of Travel*. Penguin: London.

Defoe, Daniel (1836). *The True-born Englishman: A Satire*. Leeds.

Descartes, Rene (1984). *The Philosophical Writings of Descartes*. Translated by J. Cottingham, R. Stoothoff, and D. Murdoch. Cambridge University Press: Cambridge.

Dodge, Martin, and Chris Perkins (2015). 'Reflecting on J. B. Harley's Influence and What He Missed in "Deconstructing the Map"', *Cartographica* 50: 37–40.

Edwards, Amelia (1888). *A Thousand Miles up The Nile*. George Routledge and Sons: London.

Eijgelaar, Eke, Carla Thaper, and Paul Peeters (2010). 'Antarctic Cruise Tourism: The Paradoxes of Ambassadorship, "Last Chance Tourism" and Greenhouse Gas Emissions', *Journal of Sustainable Tourism* 18: 337–54.

Emerson, Ralph (1836). *Nature*. James Munroe & Company: Boston.

Enloe, Cynthia (2014). *Bananas, Beaches, and Bases: Making Feminist Sense of International Politics, second edition*. University of California Press: Berkeley.

Everett, Daniel L. (2005). 'Cultural Constraints on Grammar and Cognition in Piraha', *Current Anthropology* 46: 621–46.

Feingold, Mordechai (2007). 'Barrow, Isaac (1630–1677)', *Oxford Dictionary of National Biography*. <http://www.oxforddnb.com/view/article/1541>.

Fernández, Pablo Iván Azócar, and Manfred Ferdinand Buchroithner (2014). *Paradigms in Cartography*. Springer: Heidelberg.

Foglia, Marc (2014). 'Michel de Montaigne', in *The Stanford Encyclopedia of Philosophy*. Edited by Edward N. Zalta. <https://plato.stanford.edu/archives/spr2014/entries/montaigne/>.

Foot, Philippa (1967). 'The Problem of Abortion and the Doctrine of Double Effect', *Oxford Review* 5: 5–15.

Foxe, Luke (1635). *North-west Fox, or Fox from the Northwest Passage*. T. Fawcett and B. Alsop: London.

Fussell, Paul (1980). *Abroad: British Literary Travelling between the Wars*. Oxford University Press: New York.

Fussell, Paul (1987). *The Norton Book of Travel*. Norton: New York.

Gerlach, Joe (2015). 'Editing Worlds: Participatory Mapping and a Minor Geopolitics', *Transactions of the Institute of British Geographers* 40: 273–86.

Ghica, Elena (1858). *Switzerland the Pioneer of the Reformation*. A. Fullarton & Co: London.

Glausser, W. (1990). 'Three Approaches to Locke and the Slave Trade', *Journal of the History of Ideas* 51: 199–216.

Goatcher, Jeff, and Viv Brunsden (2011). 'Chernobyl and the Sublime Tourist', *Tourist Studies* 11: 115–37.

Goodman, Nelson (1955). *Fact, Fiction, and Forecast*. Harvard University Press: Cambridge, MA.

Hakluyt, Richard (1889). *The principal navigations, voyages, traffiques and discoveries of the English nation*. E. & G. Goldsmid: Edinburgh.

Harley, J. B. (1989). 'Deconstructing the Map', *Cartographica* 26: 1–20.

Haviland, John B. (1998). 'Guugu Yimithirr Cardinal Directions', *Ethos* 26: 25–47.

Hayden, Judy (2012). 'Intersections and Cross-Fertilization', in *Travel Narratives, the New Science, and Literary Discourse 1569–1750*, pp. 11–24. Edited by Judy Hayden. Routledge: London.

Hooke, Robert (1665). *Micrographia*. London.

Howell, James (rep. 1869). *Instructions for Forreine Travell*. London.

Hulme, Peter (2005). 'Travelling to Write (1940–2000)', in *The Cambridge Companion to Travel Writing*, pp. 87–102. Edited by Peter Hulme and Tim Youngs. Cambridge University Press: Cambridge.

Hume, David (1739). *A Treatise of Human Nature, Book I*. London.

Ierodiakonou, Katerina, and Sophie Roux (eds) (2011). *Thought Experiments in Methodological and Historical Contexts*. Brill: Leiden.

Jacob, Christian (2006). *The Sovereign Map: Theoretical Approaches to Cartography throughout History*. Translated by Tom Conley. Edited by Edward H. Dahl. University of Chicago Press: Chicago.

Kahane, Guy (2014). 'Our Cosmic Insignificance', *Noûs* 48: 745–72.

Kant, Immanuel (2011). *Observations on the Feeling of the Beautiful and Sublime and Other Writings*. Edited by Patrick Frierson and Paul Guyer. Cambridge University Press: Cambridge.

Kingsley, Mary (2003). *Travels in West Africa*. Dover Publications: Mineola, NY.

Kitchin, R., and M. Dodge (2007). 'Rethinking Maps'. *Progress in Human Geography* 31: 331–44.

Koch, Philip (1997). *Solitude: A Philosophical Encounter*. Open Court: Chicago.

Lassels, Richard (1670). *An Italian Voyage Or A Compleat Journey Through Italy*. London.

Lee, Henry (1702). *Anti-scepticism: or, Notes Upon Each Chapter of Mr. Lock's Essay Concerning Humane Understanding*. London.

Leed, Eric J. (1991). *The Mind of the Traveller*. Basic Books: New York.

Leigh, Edward (1671). *Three Diatribes or Discourses*. London.

Littlewood, Ian (2001). *Sultry Climates: Travel and Sex since the Grand Tour*. John Murray: London.

Locke, John (1690). *An Essay Concerning Humane Understanding*. London.

Locke, John (1699). *Mr. Locke's reply to the right reverend the Lord Bishop of Worcester's answer to his second letter*. London.

Locke, John (1858). *The Life and Letters of John Locke*. Edited by Lord King. London.

Locke, John (1984). *Locke's Travels in France*. Edited by John Lough. Garland Publishers: New York.

Lopez, Barry (2014). *Arctic Dreams*. Penguin: London.

Macfarlane, Robert (2003). *Mountains of the Mind*. Granta Books: London.

Maillart, Ella (1950). 'My Philosophy of Travel' in *Traveller's Quest: Original Contributions towards a Philosophy of Travel*, pp. 114–26. Edited by M. A. Michael. William Hodge: London.

Malebranche, Nicolas (1997). *The Search after Truth*. Translated and edited by T. M. Lennon and P. J. Olscamp. Cambridge University Press: Cambridge.

Markham, Beryl (1942/1984). *West with the Night*. Virago: London.

Marshall, Tim (2016). *Prisoners of Geography*. Simon and Schuster: New York.

Mayew, William J., Christopher A. Parsons, and Mohan Venkatachalam (2013). 'Voice Pitch and the Labor Market Success of Male Chief Executive Officers'. *Evolution and Human Behavior* 34: 243–8.

Mbiti, J. S. (1969). *African Religions and Philosophy*. London: Heinemann.

McKnight, Stephen A. (2006). *The Religious Foundations of Francis Bacon's Thought*. University of Missouri Press: Columbia.

Michener, James A. (1988). *Alaska*. Fawcett Crest: New York.

Mill, J. S. (2015). On Liberty, Utilitarianism, and Other Essays. Oxford University Press: Oxford.

Milton, John (2005). *Paradise Lost*. Edited by David Scott Kastan. Hackett Publishing: Indianapolis.

Monmonier, Mark (1996). *How to Lie with Maps*. University of Chicago Press: Chicago.

de Montaigne, Michel (1845). *The Works of Montaigne, second edition*. Edited by William Hazlitt. London.

Monteith, James (1866). *First Lessons in Geography*. A. S. Barnes & Co: New York.

Moore, Richard B. (1973). 'Carib "Cannibalism": A Study in Anthropological Stereotyping', *Caribbean Studies* 13: 117–35.

More, Henry (1878). *The Complete Poems of Dr Henry More*. Edited by Alexander B. Grosart. Edinburgh University Press: Edinburgh.

More, Henry (1995). *Henry More's Manuel of Metaphysics—A Translation of the Enchiridium Metaphysicum, Vol. I*. Translated by Alexander Jacob. Georg Olms Verlag Hildesheim: Germany.

More, Thomas (1998). *Utopia*. Dover Publications: New York.

Morton, Timothy (2013). *Hyperobjects: Philosophy and Ecology after the End of the World*. University of Minnesota Press: Minneapolis.

Moulton, Ian Frederick (2000). *Before Pornography: Erotic Writing in Early Modern England*. Oxford University Press: Oxford.

Muir, John (1894/2008). *The Mountains of California*. Penguin: New York.

Muir, John (1915). *Travels in Alaska*. Houghton Mifflin: Boston.

Naess, Arne (1986). 'The Deep Ecological Movement: Some Philosophical Aspects', *Philosophical Inquiry* 8: 1–2.

Newby, Eric (1981). *A Short Walk in the Hindu Kush*. Picador: London.

Newton, Isaac (1999). *The Principia: Mathematical Principles of Natural Philosophy*. Translated by Bernard Cohen and Anne Whitman, assisted by Julia Budenz. University of California Press: Berkeley.

Newton, Isaac (2008). *The Correspondence of Isaac Newton, Volume I: 1661–1675*. Cambridge University Press: Cambridge.

Nicolson, Majorie Hope (1959). *Mountain Gloom and Mountain Glory*. Cornell University Press: New York.

Nugent, Thomas (1749). *The Grand Tour; Or, a Journey through the Netherlands, Germany, Italy, and France*. London.

Nye, David E. (1994). *American Technological Sublime*. MIT Press: Cambridge, MA.

Oelschlaeger, Max (1991). *The Idea of Wilderness*. Yale University Press: New Haven, CT.

Oladipo, Olusegun (2004). 'Religion in African Culture: Some Conceptual Issues', in *A Companion to African Philosophy*, pp. 355–3. Edited by Kwasi Wiredu. Blackwell: Malden, MA.

Olds, Sharon (2005). *Selected Poems*. Jonathan Cape: London.

Overton, John Henry (1885). 'Barrow, Isaac (1630–1677)', in *Dictionary of National Biography, 1885–1900, Volume III*, pp. 299–305. Smith, Elder & Co: London.

Palmer, Thomas (1606). *An essay of the meanes how to make our trauailes, into forraine countries, the more profitable and honourable*. London.

Parker, Mike (2009). *Map Addict*. Collins: London.

Pascal, Blaise (2003). *Pensées*. Translated by W. F. Trotter. Dover Publications: Mineola, NY.

Passmore, John (1974). *Man's Responsibility for Nature*. Scribner's: New York.

Pepys, Samuel (2000). *The Diary of Samuel Pepys*. University of California Press: Berkeley.

Perkins, Franklin (2014). 'Wandering and Being at Home', in *Landscape and Travelling East and West*, pp. 23–34. Edited by Hans-Georg Moeller and Andrew Whitehead. Bloomsbury: London.

Peterson, Michael P. (2003). 'Maps and the Internet: An Introduction', in *Maps and the Internet*, pp. 1–16. Edited by Michael P. Peterson. Elsevier: Amsterdam.

Piggott-McKellar, Annah E., and Karen E. McNamara (2016). 'Last Chance Tourism and the Great Barrier Reef', *Journal of Sustainable Tourism* 25: 397–415.

Plato (1997). *Plato: Complete Works*. Edited by John M. Cooper and D. S. Hutchinson. Hackett: Indianapolis.

Poole, Joshua (1657). *The English Parnassus*. London.

Pugliese, P. (2006). 'Hooke, Robert (1635–1703), Natural Philosopher', in *Oxford Dictionary of National Biography*. <http://www.oxforddnb.com/view/10.1093/ref:odnb/9780198614128.001.0001/odnb-9780198614128-e-13693>.

Raban, Jonathan (1992). *The Oxford Book of the Sea*. Oxford University Press: Oxford.

Ransom, J. Ellis (1940). 'Derivation of the Word "Alaska"', *American Anthropologist* 42: 5501–1.

Relph, E. (1976). *Place and Placelessness*. Pion: London.

Rose-Redwood, Reuben (2015). 'Introduction: The Limits to Deconstructing the Map', *Cartographica* 50: 1–8.

Rousseau, Jean-Jacques (1796). *The Confessions of J. J. Rousseau, to which are appended Reveries of a Solitary Walker, Vol. II*. London.

Rousseau, Jean-Jacques (1921). *Emile or Education*. Translated by Barbara Foxley. J. M. Dent & Sons: New York.

Russell, Bertrand (2009). *The Basic Writings of Bertrand Russell*. Edited by Robert E. Egner and Lester E. Denonn. Routledge: London.

Seller, John (1670). *Atlas Maritimus*. London.

Shelley, Mary (1818/2018). *Frankenstein*. Penguin: New York.

Shelley, Mary (1844). *Rambles in Germany and Italy, in 1840, 1842, and 1843*. Edward Moxon: London.

Smith, Adam (1776). *An Inquiry into the Nature and Causes of the Wealth of Nations*. London.

Smith, Justin (2015). *Nature, Human Nature, and Human Difference: Race in Early Modern Philosophy*. Princeton University Press: Princeton, NJ.

Sokolowski, Robert (1998). 'The Method of Philosophy: Making Distinctions', *The Review of Metaphysics* 51: 515–32.

Sorensen, Roy A. (1999). *Thought Experiments*. Oxford University Press: Oxford.

Strachan, Michael (2013). 'Coryate, Thomas (*c.*1577–1617)', in *Literature of Travel and Exploration: An Encyclopedia, Vol. 1: A to F*, pp. 285–7. Edited by Jennifer Speake. Routledge: London.

Stillingfleet, Edward (1697). *The Bishop of Worcester's Answer to Mr. Locke's Letter*. London.

Strabo (1917). *Geography*. Translated by Horace Leonard Jones. Harvard University Press: Cambridge, MA.

Swann, Marjorie (2001). *Curiosities and Texts: Culture of Collecting in Early Modern England*. University of Pennsylvania Press: Philadelphia.

Talbot, Ann (2010). *'The Great Ocean of Knowledge': The Influence of Travel Literature on the Work of John Locke*. Brill: Leiden.

Theroux, Paul (2011). *The Great Railway Bazaar: By Train through Asia*. Penguin: London.

Thicknesse, Philip (1768/1770). *Useful Hints to Those who Make the Tour of France*. London.

Thomas, Emily (2018). *Absolute Time: Rifts in Early Modern British Metaphysics*. Oxford University Press: Oxford.

Thompson, Carl (2007). *The Suffering Traveller and the Romantic Imagination*. Oxford University Press: New York.

Thompson, Carl (2011). *Travel Writing*. Routledge: London.

Thoreau, Henry David (1965). *Walden and Essay on Civil Disobedience*. Airmont Publishing: New York.

Thoreau, Henry (2004). *Walden; or, Life in the Woods*. Princeton University Press: Princeton.

Twain, Mark (2010). *Innocents Abroad*. Wordsworth Classics: St Ives.

van den Abbeele, Georges (1991). *Travel as Metaphor from Montaigne to Rousseau*. University of Minnesota Press: Minneapolis, MN.

Vila, Mar, Gerard Costa, Carlos Angulo-Preckler, Rafael Sarda, and Conxita Avila (2016). 'Contrasting Views on Antarctic Tourism: "Last Chance Tourism" or "Ambassadorship" in the Last of the Wild', *Journal of Cleaner Production* 111: 451–60.

Wallis, Velma (2013). *Two Old Women*. HarperCollins: New York.

Waters, David W. (1958). *The Art of Navigation in England in Elizabethan and Early Stuart Times*. Hollis and Carter: London.

Wheeler, Sara (1997). *Terra Incognita: Travels in Antarctica*. Vintage: London.

Whewell, William (1834). 'On the Connexion of the Physical Sciences. By Mrs. Somerville', *Quarterly Review* 51: 54–68.

Whitaker, Ian (1982). 'The Problem of Pytheas' Thule', *The Classical Journal* 77: 148–64.

Whitaker, Katie (2002). *Mad Madge: The Extraordinary Life of Margaret Cavendish, Duchess of Newcastle, the First Woman to Live by her Pen*. Basic Books: New York.

Winkler, Ken (2004). 'Empiricism and Multiculturalism', *Philosophic Exchange* 34: 55–84.

Witt, Charlotte (1998). 'Form, Normativity, and Gender in Aristotle: A Feminist Perspective,' in *Feminist Interpretations of Aristotle*, pp. 118–37. Edited by Cynthia Freeland. The Pennsylvania State University Press: University Park, PA.

Wolfe, Charles (2014). 'Travel as a Basis for Atheism: Free-Thinking as Deterritorialization in the Early Radical Enlightenment', in *Motion and Knowledge in the Changing Early Modern World,* pp. 141–67. Edited by Ofer Gal and Yi Zheng. Springer: Dordrecht.

Wolff, Janet (1992). 'On the Road Again: Metaphors of Travel in Cultural Criticism', *Cultural Studies* 6: 224–39.

Wollstonecraft, Mary (1793). *A Vindication of the Rights of Woman.* J. Stockdale: Dublin.

Wollstonecraft, Mary (1889). *Letters Writing During a Short Residence in Sweden, Norway, and Denmark.* Cassell & Company: London.

Wollstonecraft, Mary (1989). *The Works of Mary Wollstonecraft.* Pickering: London.

Wood, Denis (1987). 'Pleasure in the Idea: The Atlas as Narrative Form', *Cartographica* 24: 24–46.

Wood, Denis (1992). *The Power of Maps.* Guilford Press: New York.

Wood, Denis, and John Fels (1986). 'Designs on Signs: Myth and Meaning in Maps', *Cartographica* 23: 54–103.

Wood, Maureen and Ron Kolek (2010). *A Ghost A Day: 365 True Tales of the Spectral, Supernatural, and Just Plain Scary!* Adams Media: Avon, MA.

Worl, Rosata Kaahani (2016). 'Alaska', in *The Oxford Handbook of American Indian History*, pp. 301–14. Edited by Frederick E. Hoxie. Oxford University Press: New York.

INDEX

Note: Figures and boxes are indicated by an italic '*f*' and '*b*' following the page number.

For the benefit of digital users, indexed terms that span two pages (e.g., 52–53) may, on occasion, appear on only one of those pages.

Index

Index

Index

Newby, Eric 3–5
Newton, Isaac 30, 72–3, 120, 123
Nicolson, Marjorie Hope 112–14,
    121, 123–6
non-voluntary travellers 40–1
North, Marianne 171
North Pole 88, 98–9, 99*f*
    see also *Blazing World*
        (Cavendish)
North Pole (town), Alaska 88–90
Northern Lights 128–9
Northwest Passage 98, 99*f*, 111
nuclear technology 139
Nugent, Thomas 73

*Observations upon Experimental
    Philosophy* (Cavendish) 101–7
oceans
    as infinite landscapes 111,
        121–4, 133
    sea level rise 179–80
    as sublime 133–4, 136
    warming of 179–80
Odyssey (Homer) 169
Olds, Sharon 24
'On Travel' (Bacon) 72
'On Travel' (Rousseau) 74
online maps 23–4
'An Oration concerning the Foreign
    Travels of Young Gentlemen'
    (Cavendish) 81
'An Oration Reproving Vices'
    (Cavendish) 81
Ordnance Survey, UK 20
Origin of Species, The (Darwin) 41
Orwell, George 94

Palmer, Thomas 'the Travailer' 40–1,
    69–71, 175
Paradise Lost (Milton) 133
Pascal, Blaise 196
Pepys, Samuel 96–7
*Philosophical Enquiry into the Origin
    of Our Ideas of the Sublime and
    Beautiful* (Burke) 129–31
*Philosophical Transactions of
    the Royal Society* 39

philosophy of science 3
    Cavendish's 100–8
    see also Bacon, Francis; Royal
        Society
Pillars of Hercules 33–6, 34*f*
pinkness 168–9
Pirahãs tribe, Brazil 65
Pizarro, Francisco 169
Plato 36, 49–50, 94, 144,
    152, 166
Plotinus 153
Plutarch 15
Polo, Marco 44, 60–1, 169
Poole, Joshua 112–13, 121, 176
Principal Navigations (Hakluyt) 98
Principia Mathematica
    (Newton) 120
psychological turn, in travel
    writing 85
Punch 163
Pytheas 86

Quine, W. V. 2

Raban, Jonathan 123, 125–6
Rambles in Germany and Italy
    (Shelley) 136
Ray, John 3, 41
realism 22
reflectiveness 150–1
religion 56–7, 63
    African spirituality 63
    apocalypse 36–8
    atheism 56–7, 61–3, 117–18
    Bacon's religious symbolization
        36–8
    God and nature 152, 155–6
    God and space 117–25
    innate idea of God 53–4, 61–4
    wilderness and 143–4
Robinson Crusoe (Defoe) 91–2, 92*f*,
    174–5
Rousseau, Jean-Jacques 2, 9, 73–4,
    151
Royal Geographical Society 163,
    169–70, 172, 175
Royal Society 39–45, 54, 95

Index